S.A.S.
Special Ace Supply
(Teacher)

SAS: Supply Ace Special

A Quick Brown Fox Publications Book

First published in Great Britain by Quick Brown Fox Publications in 2007; this edition published by Quick Brown Fox Publications in 2007

Copyright © Brian McCusker 2007.
Edited by Adam Kirkman.

The moral right of the author has been asserted.
All names, dates and locations have been changed to keep identities secret. The views in this book are the author's views and are not necessarily the views of Quick Brown Fox Publications.

All rights reserved. No part of this publication may be reproduced, stored in a retrieval system, or transmitted in any form or by any means, without the prior permission in writing of the publisher, nor be otherwise circulated in any form of binding or cover other than that in which it is published and without a similar condition including this condition being imposed on the subsequent purchaser.

ISBN-10 0955480434 ISBN-13 9780955480430

Cover image © Chris Goodier, 2007. Used with permission.

Quick Brown Fox Publications is an independent literary agency and publishers once known as White Horse Publications. They want to hear from first time authors so please get in touch. They'd love to hear from you. Contact them at feedback@quickbrownfoxpublications.co.uk. Please recommend this book to a friend as they'd be very grateful.
www.quickbrownfoxpublications.co.uk

S.A.S.
Special Ace Supply
(Teacher)

Brian McCusker

Published by Quick Brown Fox Publications, 2007.

SAS: Supply Ace Special

To the WGB.

"Humour is also a way of saying something serious."

T.S. Eliot

SAS: Supply Ace Special

```
Date: Monday, 11.12.06
Location:   Marchington,    somewhere
 North of Leeds
Today's Enemy: The Grand Prix
```

After teaching there for a day, I rushed home to begin writing. It was a therapeutic attempt to remain sane by getting my angst onto paper. A few paragraphs of smoking biro later, I realised that I was in the extremely unusual position of teaching across the entire age range, from Year 1 to Year 11, and across the complete range of schools, from village primary schools where the kids go home on ponies, to inner-city Comprehensives where the kids go home in police cars, and sometimes even stolen police cars.

There is no red carpet treatment when a supply teacher arrives at a school, no smell of fresh paint, no eccentric members of staff conveniently 'off sick' and no children in awe of six headed Ofsted inspectors who have the power to turn them into frog spawn. We see the school for what it is; carbuncles, fistulas, bursting pus-erupting pustules, melanomas and all. We are the invisible force that keeps education on its feet in this country, or at least on its knees. What is the condition of State education in England today? Well, if it was a house, it would be an early Victorian terrace in need of gutting.

Marchington High School. A communist enclave some forty years behind Estonia. Before Marchington, I had seen my job as belonging to the sixth circle of hell but I was wrong, I had only been operating somewhere around the first or second.

It was a poor start, the doors were locked and I was forced to stand with a cluster of fourteen-year-olds who were chewing over Saturday night's Malibu party.

'Natalie said nobody liked her, so she swallowed a handful of garlic capsules.'
'Cool.'
'Yeah. What happened?'
'She was sick in her mum's wardrobe.'

I tapped on the window at a geezer in a boiler suit who gestured either that I was about to enter a whirlpool of dissatisfaction or that the staff entrance was round the back. He disappeared anyway and I carried on waiting while the kids tried to make an impression of me in the door. Finally, a moribund caretaker appeared with a fat bunch of keys and I was pushed in.

When you are a supply teacher everyday is like the first day at school. You know nothing and bewilderment is the regular condition. I was carried down the labyrinth of passages on a river of pubescence and dumped like silt outside the office of the school secretary.

School secretaries resemble a benign aunt but I'm not fooled anymore because these women are omnipresent and omniscient. They know everybody and everything, from the workings of the latest quantum photocopier to the zeitgeist psychological methodology employed in dealing with the adolescent. Today though, she can do nothing about the power cuts which mean that the school is without heat and light. Quite common apparently, which is ironic as the school is only fifty metres away from a belching power station. At least it explains the staff's predilection for fleeces and, in one case, a commando-type ski mask.

The kids, however, provide no clue concerning the unpredictable heating system, for them it is cotton shirted business as usual because in their heads they are not hacked off teenagers in a harsh northern climate, they are beach bums with hard kerbs, grey pavements and skateboards in place of white sand, blue waves and surfboards.

'Ah, Mister Erm. You are teaching English. Elizabeth will take you there.'

Elizabeth was between forty and sixty and of average build and height. Her hair was straight and shoulder length and had once been as black as a beagle's lungs, but now only a few dark strands remained threaded through the grey as a reminder that she was once young too. Elizabeth wore the teacher's uniform of fleece (in her case, lilac) and scarf (red) pulled up to her cold, purple, broken veined nose. Regrettably, I was dressed for a temperate climate. If I'd known that the conditions were going to be extreme I could have worn the salopettes that lingered from a one-off ski trip. She had another teacher uniform on, too - her eyes told the real story, panda eyes, with so many bags under them that it looked as though she was wearing two miniature cinema curtains. It's been said that you can tell how many years a teacher has been in the profession by the number of circles under their eyes.

'Are you pleased to see me, or is that a hand warmer in your pocket?' She may have said it in the days before laughter was prohibited.

'This way,' she mumbled from underneath her scarf. 'I'll show you the staff room.'

I followed her through a series of corridors that were so dark that I almost expected her to pluck a straw torch off the wall. Staff rooms are places where the concept of interior design is unknown. This one was a particularly good example. A long, baronial style table ran down the centre of the room, piled high with a K2 of paper and a heap of curious detritus which included a genuine tin hat from World War II. If I'd delved deeper I'm sure I would have found the poor sod to whom it once belonged.

Deeper still and I would unearth cannons, sabres, pikestaffs, short swords, spears, shields, cudgels, clubs and all the other teaching paraphernalia. That table was a neat representation of the inner workings of the teachers' addled heads. It was Turner Prize material. An installation symbolising the scream for help from the downtrodden middle classes. Elizabeth quickly abandoned me for her clique, perhaps supposing that I would receive my instructions through osmosis or divine revelation. I decided not to make a nuisance of myself by asking her trivia such as who and where will I be teaching, and besides, she was busy extricating a first world war greatcoat from the table.

Usually in these situations, I try to look productive by writing a letter or making up a limerick or sketching, but the cold was getting to me and my hands were shaking. Earnest Shackleton eat your frozen heart out. This morning, I was content to just observe my fellow professionals as they prepared to go over the top yet again, faces drawn and the tension palpable. They looked hoary and battle fatigued and long overdue relief. One character was particularly intriguing. From the front, he looked scarily conventional with his attire of tweed jacket, collar and tie but when he turned around it was like, 'Hey, don't try and pigeon hole me,' as his wispy grey ponytail flapped and flicked all the way down his back.

The really disturbing aspect though was the lack of anyone under fifty. (Apart from one young woman who was already showing early signs of bloom loss. I almost called out to her, 'Run for Christ's sake, before you wither on the vine! I'll hold them back. Go! Don't worry about me, I'm done for already.')

I can observe at leisure, for the supply teacher is not just a stranger but actually invisible. I can sit in the midst of a group of teachers and remain unseen because I simply do not exist within their frame of reference. It's not their fault, though, most of them can't see through the fog of depression that permeates the staff room. So I monitor and note the assorted mannerisms and ticks and clicks of the teeth and tongue and twitches and jerks and sharp staccato movements and blinks and rapid robotic nods of the head and marvel at the contemporary ballet created by accumulative stress.

The school secretary (or S.S., hmm) arrives now and pins a large sheet of paper to the wall denoting who will be covering for whom. The teachers rise as one body and peer at the sheet like A-Level students on results day, heaving groans of anguish or sighs of relief depending on the outcome.

Eventually, after walking for miles through the gloomy labyrinth I stumble into an empty, frozen, classroom with towering ceilings, ancient sash windows, flaking paintwork and knackered, sad furniture. At least I'm not in a portacabin. Whenever I find myself heading towards a peripheral portacabin, I experience the same visceral feeling that the French aristocrats had when they rode the tumbrels to Madame Guillotine.

Usually, the work set is related to the next exam that the class will be setting. Today, there is nothing. I prefer it this way because my lessons are designed for survival in that they are differentiated by ability, which means the kids can make the work as hard or as easy as they want. For example, I begin by saying that I often teach in a 'Special School' (this gets the attention of the girls) and that last week I was working with a boy who was born with no eyes (this gets the attention of the boys.) I mention that the blind boy asked me what 'red' was and I told him buses, lips, apples, peppers, fire, tomatoes. He tells me that he's never seen any of those things and that red to him is the sound of a trumpet. I explain that his interpretation is abstract and human emotions are also abstract.

I ask if anyone can say what makes them angry. All hands go up now, mostly related to sibling angst, with a sadistic step-dad anecdote thrown in too, which I quash before finding myself in social worker territory. Next, we have a competition to see how many things they can name that are red, then green, then blue, and then yellow and I write them on the board. Finally, I hand out a sheet of plain paper and explain that they have a choice; they can either copy out the words on the board and illustrate the sheet with the items (no brainer) or write a poem concentrating on one colour and once again illustrating it. I have used the lesson a thousand times, much like a northern comedian tells the same joke touring the clubs. It always works, but today it will not see action, because Elizabeth the panda has re-appeared from behind the eucalyptus trees.

'Mr. Erm. You should be next door. *Jane Eyre*,' she says, thrusting a battered copy at me. 'Read that to them.'

Now when a matador enters a bullring he at least has a cape for protection yet I am expected to teach a Year 10 class armed only with a beat up copy of *Jane Eyre* which is hardly a substitute. I stand outside the door knowing they are in there waiting. I recognise the feeling, it's so familiar, a mix of fear and dread as the heart begins to pump adrenalin into the system, making ready for fight or flight. Unlike the cave man, I am not in a position to fight nor financially for flight.

Consequently, the adrenalin will not be used. Instead, it will be stored in my ever-hardening arteries. I can hear the noise coming from inside. The sort of stir that caused various body fluids to stream from the Christians prior to facing five famished tigers and a barbarous Scythian wielding the jawbone of an ox. Like the Christians, I pray that I have still have a modicum of presence after twenty years of combat. After all, I am six feet four and looking particularly smart in a bright orange Versace shirt (ten pounds from Oxfam, shh) with dark blue suit and red silk tie embroidered with a seasonal 'Merry Christmas.'

I push open the door and the scene is a TV movie featuring a Bronx High School where the kids sit on desks sharpening chair legs with flick-knives. My presence is ineffectual. Maybe I really am invisible. I am mentally entertaining myself with the advantages of being invisible when the very apologetic panda arrives. I am in the wrong classroom again. A few minutes later, I enter the correct classroom with my metaphorical fists flailing ready to let them know just who the hell has the strongest smelling piss round here. My build up of adrenaline is wasted though as this particular class are quite docile.

'*Jane Eyre*. We are and must be one and all burdened with faults in this world but the time will soon come when I trust we shall put them of in putting off our corruptible bodies; when debasement and sin will fall from us with this cumbrous frame of flesh and only the spark of the spirit will remain the impalpable principle of life and thought pure as when it left the Creator to inspire the creature…aaaarghhh!' I feel like I'm in the movie *Speed*. If I stop reading *Jane Eyre*, a fifty-pound bomb will go off.

Break time and back to the staff room to watch the pony-tailed one gnaw on a frozen pork pie, the steam of his breath creating the illusion that it is piping hot. Coffee is served from a trolley along with greasy sausage rolls and crisps: teenage junk food. The ancients clap their hands to force heat into their extremities. I remain standing as the factions have already formed and are linked like chain mail against any possible intrusion from a member of another department or worse, a complete unknown, and potential virus.

I reckon it all started going down the chute when crockery was abolished in the school canteens and the teachers found themselves eating off plastic trays with custard from the dessert dimple slopping over the gravy groove. The government must then have thought, 'shit, if they will stand for that, they will stand for anything, put their pay on hold and run down the infrastructure until it rots.'

'But what if they complain, sir?'

'Then let them eat their cake with a plastic spoon.'

I am just about to delve into the rubble pile on the table to examine a canubic jar when a wild-eyed woman lunges towards me.

'It's you,' she says. 'St. Boswells High, twenty years ago.'

God, it's Maggie. Madder than ever. She must be nearly seventy.

'I should be retired,' she says. 'But my fecking daughter is pregnant again with no man.'

I assume she means that her daughter's pregnancy is the result of a brief fling but you never know with mad Maggie, it could be a pronouncement of the second coming. I could respond but there is no point. Maggie speaks at the speed of an Uzi sub-machine gun but never listens to a word in reply. You could tell her that you had just been gang buggered by aliens and she would respond with a story about her hamster chewing the curtains. It turns out that she is now the drama teacher here, which causes me to have a flashback. Maggie continues to mow me down but - cue the harp music and wavy lines - I am now in Grayson College in Leeds, recalling the day when I was asked to teach the same subject.

I am in the drama 'suite', a room that could be used as an aircraft hangar for a jumbo jet. I feel dangerously small and I have never taught drama in my life. I look around the hangar, looking for clues on how to teach the Stanislavsky method, but there is more chance of finding a joystick and some landing gear. The breezeblock stadium of darkness is bare apart from a dozen plastic chairs, which will soon gain in importance. The lessons are an hour and a half, the length of a football match. Two minutes to nine. What will the first class be like? Will they be cool like James Dean? Will there be a Dustin Hoffman type who believes in getting into role? A Marilyn, who, though gorgeous to look at, has difficulty with her lines? A laconic Bogart oozing with presence? A young smouldering Brando ready to turn it on when required? A dangerous Jack Nicholson? A grinning Tom Cruise? Hey, this could be good. Nine o'clock and the doors rupture. All shapes and sizes make their entrance stage left, stage right and stage middle. A rich ethnic mix from Hollywood to Bollywood.

'It's another one,' yells a huge West Indian girl. 'We get a new mother every week.'

Fifteen boys and twelve girls take up their positions for a rerun of *Grand Prix*, with the girls taking on the role of ululating crowd and the boys climbing into their throbbing racing cars for ten laps of Monaco.

The flag is raised and they are off. Pushing the plastic chairs backwards now with their feet, the screech of metal on concrete is ear splitting and the crowd scream for their champion. One circuit of the hangar complete, the screech of tyres, the smell of burning rubber, feet ramming the floor pedals, travelling anti-clockwise, in reverse, like my whole world is in freefall. I look at my watch: 9.05am. Just another one hour twenty-five minutes to go. Round they go again for the second lap. Chair number six appears to be in the lead but only just from chair number ten who is trying to cut inside him on the tight bend. Chair number seven is coming up fast, thighs bulging, and trainers smoking. Lap three and chair number six is going round the outside. Shit! He's not going to make it. Over and over he tumbles and the plastic works model chair slams heavily into the breeze block. Miraculously he's up on his feet. A little dazed but that's all and he gets right back in the seat. It's the only way, if you don't get right back on, you could lose your nerve and never be able to push a chair at speed around a drama studio again.

My brain is shrieking at me. The pain has penetrated and I have to make a choice. I can run out of the double doors or I can bring down the chequered flag. The first option is tasty but I take the second. I run onto the track and stop the race. There is a massive protest but to no purpose, the race is stopped and I begin to shout at 120 decibels and just fall short of calling them a pack of bastards. I tell them to stand against the wall so I can keep an eye on them. I don't want anyone behind me. They shuffle over to the breezeblock, some drag their chairs and sit on them and that's fine.

I tell them who I am. They are not impressed but I tell them anyway.

The shouting has the effect of pumping me up to three or four times my normal size but I am using all of my strength just to keep a lid on this one. I can feel gaskets popping. If I stop talking, I'm dead. I tell them to form a circle and then before they become a collective conscience again I have them running and weaving in and out of it. The big West Indian girl will not have it though. She stands at the back with her arms folded across her chest making sucking noises with her teeth. I don't blame her, it is beneath her dignity to move faster than walking pace. I put the others into groups and give them ten minutes to work out a routine that will create a machine from their individual staccato movements. They get involved, they are even giggling, and the large girl taps her foot in the corner.

'Ok, let me see what you have come up with.'

The first three efforts are begrudgingly delivered but the fourth group seem keen, one boy and three girls. The girls form a pyramid while the boy executes a series of Arab springs before bouncing over the top of them. It isn't exactly what I asked for but it sure is spectacular.

I look at my watch. The hands of time are frozen. I am already mentally and physically deranged and there is still over an hour of the lesson left. I organize them into groups again and try some relay racing. The drama lesson is quickly taking on the look of a PE session but who cares, they are still involved, apart from the West Indian girl who when asked to perform a squat thrust, a star jump and five press ups gives me an extra strong suck and folds her arms ever tighter.

Forty minutes left, they are warmed up now and I have to keep them from getting back on the race track. One or two already look twitchy and have given the accelerator a quick thrust to test my reaction.

'Form another circle. We are going to pretend to pass a ball to each other, first the ball is made of glass, don't drop it. This time the ball is made of lead and you can hardly lift it, brilliant, now as light as a feather, excellent.'

Meanwhile, I am writing a list of activities on pieces of scrap paper. Window cleaning, kite flying, dog walking, pancake making, anything, for one to mime and the others to guess. It works, another ten minutes have passed, twenty to go. The West Indian girl has disappeared.

'You have all seen soap operas. I want you to spend ten minutes working out a scene from your favourite one where someone has gone missing. Spread out, discuss and rehearse and then perform it.'

The results are not brilliant, mostly concerning scenes of ultra violence and extreme anger, but they have made an effort and I thank them. They don't hear me though and with a shout of 'wanker!' they are gone and I am slumped against the ropes in the knowledge that in ten minutes I will have to do it all again with a different group.

At lunchtime I found a pub and drank two pints of beer and smoked four cigarettes. Food, I could not stomach, for I knew that soon I would have to do it all again for another one and half hours.

For the final lesson of the day, I am asked to support the media studies teacher. She looks wrecked beyond repair and has the panda eyes associated with the profession. I watch in growing sadness as she goes through her lesson. The kids don't even bother to remove their coats. For the next hour, they talk amongst themselves and generally arse around while she carries on with her lesson as if she is addressing twelve attentive pupils at Winchester Public School. At the end of the lesson, I ask her what effect such lessons have on her personality.

'I have no personality,' she says, staring through and past me.

Later, when I'm getting my form signed, the Deputy Head tells me that I've done a good job and asks if I would be interested in teaching drama full time, starting tomorrow. I could have said, 'phone my agent,' but in truth, I was too beat up for any quips. All I wanted now was to go home and crawl under the bed with my favourite pillow and a bottle of whisky with a rubber teat on the end of it.

After more harp music and wavy lines, I'm back at Marchington, and Maggie is gibbering about a café she bought which went up in flames and took her life savings with it. Another failed escape bid, another tunnel discovered by those pervasive prison guards. The cold is penetrating now. Sweat has turned to ice and my nose is streaming. I might have to slot someone for their fleece; it's them or me.

Some interesting and topical work has been left for the next class. An improvement on *Jane Eyre,* anyway. The content of the lesson is on printed A3 sheets and involves a magazine piece on a famous model who has achieved great things despite having her legs amputated below the knee. Cool, but not cool enough for the boys at the front who keep a-slippin' and a-slidin' off their chairs. After a suitable rebuke, I carry on reading the article hoping they will get into the spirit of the story. There are even juicy quotes from Frank Zappa, such as 'there is nothing sexier than tits and muscle,' but no go, falling off chairs is more appealing. I carry on though, determined to make sure the kids who want to learn get the opportunity, for that is my teaching ethos.

'Stop shouting for God's sake! You are giving me a bad head.'

I turn to a girl in hat, gloves and muffler.

'Excuse me?'

'Stop shouting,' she says. 'Or I'm off.'

'If I'm speaking loud,' I protest, 'it is to overcome certain people who are making my job very difficult.'

'That's it, I'm bored and I'm off.'

And at that she stands up, pushes by me, steps over the boys on the floor and walks out.

Brilliant.

'Take no notice of her, sir,' says a girl in the middle row, 'she's weird. Or them either,' she continues, pointing with distain at the heap of acne wriggling on the floor, 'they are just morons. Let's get on with the lesson, I'm enjoying this.'

The others mutter in agreement and I oblige because it pisses me off that a few can wreck the education of the many. It is the reason why in the big cities of America, state schools are called 'poor man's schools' and why anyone with an average salary pays for their child to have an education in a school where disruption by a minority is not tolerated.

It will happen here, it's on the way: it has to be.

One of the biggest problems with supply teaching is that I know nothing of individual personalities or circumstances or the reason young Jason keeps falling off his chair is because last week his father was electrocuted after spending two years on death row for a crime he didn't commit. Another difficulty is that the regular teachers know the Darrens before they have gained five feet in height, eight stone in weight, several body piercings and an attitude. Consequently, their overall perception of the Darrens is a mixture of beast and little boys blue, which affords them a strong psychological advantage in dealing with their hormonal aberrations, whereas I only see the beast. By the end of the lesson, I am red faced and hot and all the classic symptoms are there - palpitations, clenching and unclenching of fists, high blood pressure, dry mouth and clamminess - so I go in search of their form teacher to take a big bite from her arse. When I find her, she is sitting at her desk with a pile of unmarked exercise books, head in one hand and pen in the other and I think, does she really need a raging bull to cope with as well? Like she needs a colostomy bag. I let the matter rest.

Lunch time. I have to get out even if it's just to thaw. I get in my car and put the heater on but it only blows out more cold air. I drive, just drive, anywhere and find myself in the town centre in a traffic jam. By the time I have extricated myself and eaten an icy banana it's time for the afternoon lessons to start but at least I have managed to avoid the staff room, that limbo land of despair, and mad Maggie.

I used to whinge about teaching but not anymore. Grumbling is a coping mechanism that can keep you in the same undesirable position for a lifetime. My thinking now is - if you don't like it, don't do it. Or at least look for an alternative - but please don't sit around saying how crap everything is: leave, get out, make the great quantum leap of faith. I keep telling myself the same but most times I see myself as someone hanging onto a splitting branch while a river swirls about my legs and hips. I am unable to pull myself out but I can't let go either. Perhaps if I just let go I will find myself surging through wild white water but then, who knows, I may round a bend and find myself in a sweet meadow where cows are black and white and bees go hum.

The next lesson is with Year 11. My instructions are one word, 'Macbeth.' I sort out a few illustrated copies and while waiting for the class to arrive I try to keep warm by running on the spot. It's a small class but there is always a reason for that. Ten boys and one girl, Sarah, who chews gum like an extra in an amateur production of *Grease*.

I introduce myself; a tradition more than a necessity, and hand out the books.

'We'll read Act two, Scene two. Who'll be Lady Macbeth?'

I stare at Sarah and she takes the hint.

It's going well. Macbeth and his Lady have performed the dreadful deed and the gum chewer is doing fine. Macbeth is causing problems though, he is murdering the play as well as the king with his monotone rendition of the speeches.

'For God's sake,' I say. 'Give it passion.'

He pushes the text across his desk, folds his arms and pouts his lip.

'Anyone else want to read the part of Macbeth?' I ask.

No response, so it's left to me and Sarah to carry the scene.

'Your turn, Lady Macbeth.'

'Who was it that thus cried? Why worthy Thane,
You do unbend your noble strength, to think
So brainsickly of things... Fuck off!'

I'm sure the sullen former Thane of Cawdor was involved in her outburst but I was forced to send her out. That was the end of the reading because, even though most teachers are frustrated actors, I am not being paid enough to take on all the roles. By now, it's too dark to read the words anyway.

When they leave, I wait for the last class of the day but ten minutes later, no-one has arrived and it's becoming bleaker by the minute.

Usually, I see my role as a pilot whose job is to fly the plane, land it safely and go home. The big advantage of supply teaching is that you don't have to deal with meetings, parents, politics, staff rooms, senior management, government initiatives, ineffective trade unions and planning ad infinitum. Today though, I am strapping on my parachute and standing over a frozen wing as I am completely out of fuel.

Date: Tuesday, 12.12.06
Location: Hiatus
Today's Enemy: mounting bills

I can't face working today, not after yesterday so when the phone rings I ignore it and feel guilty and apprehensive at the thought of losing money. It rings again but I bite on the pillow and refuse to answer it. Ten minutes later, it rings again, and my insecurities come swimming to the surface whispering, 'arches, blankets, meths, penny whistles and plastic cups.' Actually, the idea of begging for a living sometimes seems a more attractive proposition than spending the day in a box with a lot of kids who want you to cough up blood and die. I remember one particularly nasty icy morning when the rain was drilling through the windscreen driving past a huddle of half drowned navvies and thinking, 'lucky bastards.'

The phone rings again and I clasp my right wrist with my left hand to prevent my arm snaking over and picking it up. The agency knows I'm there, and the ringing persists, urging me to answer because without me, they cannot exist.

Agencies. There are good ones and there are parasites that suck you dry leaving you an underpaid husk while they grow fat. Ideally, a supply teacher should work for the local council because that way they are paid to scale and have access to the teachers' pension scheme. Agencies do not contribute towards pensions. The second best option is to work with an agency that pays to scale and does not penalise you for being more expensive than a new graduate. It is easy to be cynical but reality insists that the more they have to pay you the less they earn for themselves. However, there is an increasing number of schools and situations that demand a heap of experience in the same way that you wouldn't give a first year junior doctor a heart transplant operation to perform. Some agencies, though, have not grasped this and insist on sending teachers with limited experience to cover a class of kids that gobble them up and shit them out in perfectly round pellets.

The agency you never want to work for is the one that pays you a rock bottom rate. I was recently offered the same as I was earning ten years ago. Their chunk is outrageous. They are charging the schools something in the region of two hundred pounds a day and offering the teachers less than half that. There are days when I have been offered work in five different schools on the same day. If I could clone myself, I would be in serious money. Of course, this is the principle behind the agencies. I know of an ex-Headteacher who retired a couple of years ago to set up an agency which effectively means he is earning from every teacher he sends out. He now has five hundred on his books. That's serious money, with no great unwashed masses in sight. Now that's intelligence!

If you really have to be a supply teacher, then the best option is to become known to three or four schools. This will guarantee full time work at top drachma. It is also better for the schools because then they have continuity and no agency fees. So get a good CV, a couple of sound referees and, if you are called into a school that you like, then smile a lot and be as flexible as hot toffee. It also pays to learn three chords on a guitar. Over the years, I have made more money than Donovan ever did from his song *Colours*.

The phone rings again but I still can't answer it. I wonder if it's due to depression. Is it the job that depresses me? Or is it because I suffer from depression that I do the job? Am I depressed? Perhaps not, but there are times when the prospect of teaching in yet another unknown school is like being pressed between two stone slabs. Eventually it stops ringing and it's past eight thirty, I should be safe now, although I have been called at ten-o-clock. That's unusual though and I can feel the slabs being lifted.

It is rare not to be working but the feelings I get as I wander slowly down the stairs are full of pleasure and pleasantry and warmth and happy childhood memories of throwing a sickie and spending a day playing with toy soldiers in front of a coal fire. Perhaps it's necessary to experience the lows in order to appreciate the highs. It's a familiar theory, like participating in extreme sports to really understand the joy of existence.

So it was that I ordered a pot of breakfast Darjeeling in a quaint little tea shop around 10.15, just about the time when I would have been going out for a stint of yard duty - which is something else about supply teaching, it's always somehow your turn for yard duty.

I find yard duty totally emasculating. It is like taking an axe to your self-worth and cutting a v-shaped wedge in it prior to taking up a chainsaw to do the felling job properly. There you are, a middle aged man, cold and dispossessed, towering above the kids, as footballs hit you in the face and tiny girls look up at you with tears streaming down their grief-stricken faces over the fact that Leanne has called them a pig.

In comprehensive schools, it's the big girls who cry because Darren has stolen their smokes and called Jasmine a slag. Whatever, it's a nightmare and probably the most spiritually depleting aspect of the job.

I pour tea from a white china pot into a cup and saucer with Margaret, my partner of five years, who has taken an hour off work to share the experience with me. She is a book restorer and works more or less in peaceful solitude all day, but she too has her stressful moments. Sometimes there is static interference when she is listening to the afternoon play. Is no one immune?

I pour in the milk and enjoy the simplicity of white table cloths and bland inoffensive music, put cup to lip and taste the hot tea, picked from the foothills of the Himalayas. Marchington is fading satisfactorily into the past and I am very much in the present, this precise moment, and it is beautiful and almost, but not quite, worth the incursion into hell to experience this almost unbearable lightness of being.

SAS: Supply Ace Special

**Date: Wednesday, 13.12.06
Location: Cherry Grove, somewhere in the Bradford desert
Today's Enemy: portacabins**

7.30am. I have been up since 6am. When the phone rings I have to be mentally alert and physically prepared to scramble. I feel a bit stronger today after my petite recuperation. A nice little primary school would be nice, a Year 4, for it's the age when children haven't yet developed cynicism. With Year 4 kids, you can make up stories and they do not have to suspend disbelief, they just believe.

As an introduction to creative writing, I tell the story of how my mum and I received a gas bill for £2000. In order to pay it I had to sell my car, but on the way to the garage I was given a smelly football sock full of broken glass by a strange looking man who told me to bury it in the garden and leave it overnight.

The story has developed organically over the telling to the point where I could almost take it on the road as a mini one man pantomime, with the frustrated actor in me taking on the roles of 'strange man', 'gormless son' and 'tetchy mother' all with different accents, usually a Glaswegian, a Brummie and a Geordie, although there has been the occasional Eastender and Aussie thrown in too.

The Year 4 kids sit open mouthed as I explain about the giant glass tower and the glass giant and the diamonds in the glass tower that I filled my cargo trouser pockets with and my mum hitting the scary giant with a sledge hammer and him splintering into a million pieces - 'and have you ever been out driving with your parents at night and seen the shiny lights in the middle of the road?'

'Yes! Yes! Cat's eyes. Cat's eyes!'

'That's what some people call them but really they are bits of the glass giant.'

'Gasp!' Eyes wide - mouths open.

By Year 5 the kids keep interrupting with a few asking, 'is this true?' By Year 6 they say, 'that's not true,' but still the hint of a question remains in the statement.

I tried the same story recently in a Comprehensive school with a Year 8 class with the intention of getting them to update an old fairy tale. It was like trying to perform *The Seagull* to a group of drunken football fans. By the time I got to the bit where the shards of broken glass grow into a giant glass tower, I was fending off the verbal equivalent of ripe tomatoes and half empty beer tins.

Alas, the Year 4 class in a pleasant little primary school is not to be. I answered the phone with my super-positive voice, ready to go anywhere, anytime, no questions asked. Agencies like that, it means they don't have to waste those golden minutes between half seven and eight. Your Special Ace Supply teacher asks no questions. Information is supplied on a need no know basis only and that amounts to the name of the school and the address. The rest can be found out upon engaging the enemy.

Cherry Grove High School. It sounds exotic but it's not. 'It's pretty tough,' they warn me. I want to ask, 'how tough?' but there is no real answer to that one. Besides, I need the money, for in the ruthless world of supplying, if you don't work you don't eat, it is teaching without a safety net but that's still better than having to endure staff meetings.

I leave for work early because the road is a well used single carriageway that is usually blocked by a malevolent farmer in a muck spreader. A few miles down the A road, I turn off for Cherry Grove and see the smoke plumes rising from various navy blue clusters of kids heading in the same direction.

The school secretary is a clone of the last school; someone is churning them out somewhere, the fiend. She is portly and efficient and focused on unwrapping her first fudge of the day. I am to teach Spanish and the first lesson is with the bottom set.

'The bottom set,' she repeated, a sliver of caramel coloured saliva cascading down the left side of her mouth, 'teaching Spanish in the portacabins.'

Ah shit. The treble. The holy trinity of supply misery: a bottom set, a foreign language and a portacabin.

Portacabins: n. Latin.

> *Horrible, rotting wooden chalets on the periphery of a school. Freezing boxes where litter swirls like tumbleweed. Monuments to the neglect of State Education. A wilderness of low and under achievers banished to far flung outposts where the job of the teacher is one of containment.*

In portacabins, the children of another God can make as much noise as they like, they can (and do) howl at the moon. In portacabins, no-one can hear you scream. Built ostensibly as temporary adjuncts thirty years ago, they still stand and mock all pretence of an egalitarian education system.

It is my job to keep the banished contained in this extended coffin for an hour. If no-one escapes during that time then I have performed my duty. I will repeat the task throughout the day. No-one must escape. Hold the line.

I examine the work that has been set. 'Year 10 - Translate your timetable into Spanish.' Bollocks! I feel like Nelson peering through his telescope, one foot on a rusty spiked cannon and seeing a French flotilla of aircraft carriers armed with nuclear warheads and vials of botulism heading his way.

I read the instructions again, but the words remain the same:

'Translate your timetable into Spanish.'

My left eye is flickering already and the stinking crate is still empty of enemy. No. It's time to delve into my personal survival kit of plain A3 paper, coloured pencils, stencils, and information sheet on 'How Bees Make Honey.' The class will then make their own information sheet about bees using mine as a guideline. That will keep them busy, it always does. Ten minutes later, the bottom set enter like a murder of crows and, after establishing territorial rights, they eventually settle down and work peacefully and even productively. Lovely.

The following lesson is Religious Education with Year 7 in the bit of school made of bricks and mortar and not compressed straw and mud. The RE brief is brief too, 'Discuss the existence of God in terms of the 'Great Designer' theory.' This is more like it. It could so easily have read, 'Translate the Ten commandments into Hebrew,' but no, here is the chance to discuss ontological issues with a group of 11-year-olds.

They arrive quietly and look smart, no hangman's noose ties, no flapping shirt tails, all shining faces and bright eyes, and for the next hour I talk and they listen and they talk and I listen and we shoot off at mighty tangents related to all matters religious.

Looking back, that class were incredible, they gushed with ideas and they listened politely while these were exchanged. When they left I felt quite high, a feeling I remembered from my past as being a regular occurrence. I had imparted knowledge; I wasn't a policeman, a social worker, a faceless outsider, or a jailer, but a teacher, a conduit for knowledge, a beacon lighter. I suddenly remembered how much I used to enjoy teaching, especially when I was in my mid-twenties when the staff room was full of young people all up for a laugh and a party.

My first post happened by accident but it lasted a year and is the one I remember the most fondly. I had just finished training and was on the county supply list. I was sharing a flat at the time with a couple of strangers when I received a call from a Headmaster concerning a temporary position teaching Craft,

Design and Technology at his Grammar School. My knowledge of CDT was limited to a garden dibber I had made in woodwork ten years ago, but I don't suppose Michael Caine had ever fired a Lee Enfield rifle when he got the part in *Zulu*.

The school was 15 miles away and, as I didn't have a car, I cycled there. On the way, the oily, greasy bike chain enmeshed itself with the gears, which took me half an hour to extricate. I arrived with five minutes to spare, lathered in sweat, and was received by the Head, a studious looking old gent who showed me to a magnificent oak panelled room. He shook hands and gave me an enquiring look. We took afternoon tea and spoke of many things, none of which were related to CDT, which was considerate of him. He insisted on calling me Graham but I let it go. He was particularly impressed with the fact that I worked part-time for the Theatre because he was treasurer of the Gilbert and Sullivan Society.

After swapping a few theatre stories, and listening to him sing 'I am the very model of a modern Major General,' he shook my hand again and offered me the job. I cycled home in a dream-like state. When I finally arrived at my flat and glanced in the mirror I understood then why his first glances at me had been so curious, for I was smudged from forehead to chin with a thick cake of oil that must have been present throughout the interview.

Now I realised why he hadn't bothered to ask me anything relating to the job, he had assumed that I was a veritable Henry Straker, the 'New Man' of Shaw's 'Man and Superman', one of the burgeoning mechanically minded, so recently empowered, working class, a would-be usurper of the establishment and the classically learned. He must have reckoned that his MA in Greek and Latin would soon be found wanting in the new fangled world of cogs and gear ratios. Better, then, to avoid the subject altogether. Ideally, I would have been wearing a boiler suit, cloth cap, and spotted 'kerchief with a monkey wrench in my back pocket and a spanner at the ready. I was to start the following Monday. It was still only Wednesday and still time for the cavalry to arrive just in time to save me. The cavalry, as usual, never came and so I embarked on a learning curve that was so arched that I would often meet myself going the other way.

Somehow, I stayed there for a year and had a brilliant time. I even made a chess board. A week or so later, it transpired that Graham, one of the lads in the flat, was also a newly qualified teacher and by an amazing coincidence actually had a degree in CDT and was also on the county supply list.

Lunch at Cherry Grove High. A different staff room, same set up. A selection of dodgy chairs guaranteed to annihilate the lumbar region. Empty, apart from a couple of support staff. They do have a water cooler, though. I didn't stay, instead I drove out into the country and parked in a lane. It was warm for the time of year, bright yellow sunshine and a pale blue sky over flat, bare fields. I closed my eyes and felt the pump of my heart beating too fast. I forced myself to breathe slowly, closed my eyes and fell asleep for twenty minutes. I am good at this now. It is something I perfected in my recent 'Deer Hunting' teaching days; I am referencing the film, not the 'sport.' I call them my 'Deer Hunting' days because of the amount of mental torture to which I was subjected.

It has been one of the hottest autumns on record and today the sun is hammering into the south facing classroom, a veritable glass box with no blinds or curtains for protection against its cruel glare. Because it is autumn, the central heating is hissing too and the rusty windows won't budge. It is cloying and hellishly hot and the Year 8 I am trying to teach are complaining of feeling sick. Meanwhile, I am regretting that slice of pizza I had for lunch, the slice with the pair of anchovies on it.

The sun raises the temperature into the tropics, my stomach is expanded, a bloated feeling that is happening more and more so that I just want to take my shirt off and open the buttons on my waist band and just flop across a few desks like a beached whale. Christ, what is happening to me? When I was teaching CDT, I was cycling fifteen miles to work and going for a four-mile run at lunchtime. I am way past my sell-by date now and will surely die in harness. Meanwhile, I struggle through the bone-hacking ennui of watching *Teletubbies* while the class make notes on the format in order to discover what makes it so successful. Just when you thought the job has bottomed out, I find I am analysing the seemingly consequential antics of Tinkywinky and Lala whilst becoming more and more convinced that the life I am leading is not my own and that I am merely the plaything of some malevolent god. Finally, the hands of the clock drag themselves round to the penultimate bell of the day.

The Year 10 kids try to enter as the Year 8 kids try to leave, causing a scrum in the door and a bottleneck with me in the middle.

'Excuse me, can we get out first?'

'No!' Replies a surly 15-year-old girl with long blonde hair and a face already etched with hard lines around her naso-labial furrows so that by the time she is in her mid-twenties she will be wearing what the plastic surgeons call a 'marionette.' I would have admonished her, but I was as dry as a camel's arse and needed water badly.

The final lesson is to supervise Year 11 in the cookery block. When I arrive, the class are recreating a scene from the kitchens of *Ghormenghast*. Things are happening though, dough is kneaded, flour mixed, eggs beaten and all I have to do is make sure that the lesson remains *Teletubbies* and does not descend into *Sooty and Sweep*.

I will be subtle, like a Victorian butler inspecting the downstairs on the afternoon before a particularly important dinner. The girls are oblivious to my presence, adding to my theory that I am now invisible. As if to prove the point, a tall statuesque blond leans over the table in front of me, stretches her already arse cheek hugging trousers even tighter and says, 'look Sarah, no knicker line. I'm wearing a thong!'

3.30pm. Beautiful. Another day, another dollar. I hate wishing time away, it's such a precious commodity, but teachers are very good at it. I remember one bloke who should have been arrested for crimes to chronology. He was full of outbursts such as, 'Brilliant, it's Wednesday lunchtime, tomorrow is Thursday and then it's Friday and then it's the weekend and then it's half term in three weeks and only another ten to the summer holidays, that's only fifty days if you don't include the weekends.' Then it's just another ten thousand, four hundred and twenty six days until we are in our pine box. Yippee!

SAS: Supply Ace Special

Date: Thursday, 14.12.06
Location: St. Boswells High, somewhere in war-torn Leeds
Today's Enemy: 9X

I appear to have found myself a regular slot, two days a week at an inner city school in Leeds, but not just any inner city school, this is St. Boswells High School, and for some reason my existence has become inextricably linked with it. I was there twenty years ago and, more recently, six years ago. Grim, grimmer and now grimmest? I can't seem to escape the place, it washes into my life at irregular intervals, like black coal onto the beach of my home town. It's like I'm caught in a big circular current. I get carried far away and consider I am heading towards far distant exotic shores, safe from its tidal pull, only to find myself washed up there again.

First impressions are important. The entrance is a swirling tumbleweed of crisp packets and litter. This school has its own seagull colony that feed and survive off all the detritus left behind after break times. These birds don't look much like their coastal cousins though, their plumages are spotty and they look pale.

I have been teaching here for six weeks now and the situation is surreal. I am teaching English, leastways that is my title but once again, like all forms of warfare, the name of the game is survival. The premise from the point of view of the English department is one of don't bother us and we won't bother you. Consequently, I see no one from the department at all. For all they know I could be sitting naked in the middle of a chalk drawn pentangle daubed in chicken blood, wearing a freshly sacrificed goat's head.

The history of the post is a familiar one. Their regular teacher reaches the age of fifty, having spent twenty-five years at the chalk face, and his Head is screaming out to him that he's done enough for society and that for the sake of his sanity he needs to get out. A couple of years ago, this was allowed, but recently early retirement has ended or as some put it, 'the bastards closed the gates.' This was partly due to teachers, once they hit fifty, getting out faster than shit off a stick.

'Close the frigging gates quick!' Came the cry, 'the schools are haemorrhaging!'

And all the poor bastards who were forty nine blinked in horror as the mighty grey iron gates slammed closed for another ten years, locking them in while their friends who were fifty waved from the other side, golf clubs already strapped across their back.

Now the only way out is to play the stress card and hope that you are shell shocked and disturbed enough to get a ticket out, otherwise it's six months on full pay and six months on half pay and then zilch as even the paltry pension is frozen, all twenty five eightieths of it, more Bollinger, anyone? So unofficially, the regular English teacher will not be back but officially, he still works there and so an army of supply teachers have stood in front of his former classes to be picked off at will by the sniping kids.

The latest in a long line of fall guys is me and I laugh because life is teaching me a lesson: it is telling me that a person who refuses to change their lives will reap the consequences. In this case, condemned to wander for all eternity through the corridors of St. Boswells High School as punishment for cowardice and for refusing to jump off the spinning hamster wheel while I still could. The gods must have laughed loud when they heard the agency offering me the job at St. Boswells High and loudest of all when they heard me accept.

I drove to Leeds gripping hard on the steering wheel, cod eyed and expressionless, unable to fully accept that I was going back. It didn't seem right. I was flouting natural laws; a person should only ever have to go to St. Boswells once and then move on. It is a school to make your mistakes in and leave. After St. Boswells, any school would seem like a dreamscape. It's the teacher's equivalent of a soldier's stint in Afghanistan, a place to earn your stripes before moving onto a cosier billet, but I haven't moved on and so it's back to St. Boswells for a third tour of duty.

I am introduced to the Head of the English department, a tiny woman around the sixty mark. She shows me to a room that's far away from the rest of the department and that is the induction over, apart from, 'If you need any paper ask Mrs. Wilder.' The ripped wallpaper is the colour of diarrhoea, grey net curtains hang in tatters from the windows and the carpet is threadbare and stained. I examine the view from the filthy unwashed windows, a muddy and littered knoll behind which stand several ash coloured tower blocks framed by a rainbow that surely must be out there somewhere just as long as you have sunshine in your heart.

I look at the register for my first class. Sixteen names, Year 10: all boys, not a good sign. I decide to play it safe and let the bees make honey. The boys arrive and I give out the bee sheet and ask them to have a go at making a similar one. There are only ten of them; six are in court. They look at the sheet and then ask for pencils. Pencils. Eighty per cent of the kids don't carry a pencil in this school which causes head numbing disruption. I solve the problem by purchasing two hundred pencils out of my own money, it's not the final solution but it nicely counters their opening gambit of, 'how can I fucking work without a pencil?'

Over the weeks I have been at St. Boswells I have made efforts to be sociable but the English Department has the feel of a coven about it. The all female staff box themselves into a tiny room during break. I sat with them once, but one of the coven went on and on about the discharge from her vagina as if she was discussing the best way to bake a light sponge. I have also tried the staff room, but it's stiflingly hot and usually empty apart from a couple of fat bearded blokes who trough their lunch from a plastic tray. There is also a windowless room in there, a box within a box, a walk in wardrobe. I discovered it only when the door opened and I thought, 'shit, the building is on fire' as huge billowing clouds of smoke emerged alongside a corpulent coughing woman in a mustard coloured cardigan. The door closed again then and, curious, I looked through the glass panel in the door to see a dozen people smoking: a veritable human kipper box. 'Gas! Gas! - Quick boys, an ecstasy of fumbling.'

The next class are called 9X. The previous class was called 10X, maybe there is a 9 triple X that no-one gets to hear about. They live up to their X rating soon enough and my first impression is one of size, some of these kids are enormous.

What the hell happens to them between eleven and fourteen? I know that puberty plays its part but some of these kids, especially the girls, are like parodies of American wrestlers, the mean ones, with voices and attitudes to match. Big Estelle looks like she runs her own pub on a tough estate and is making a good fist of it, 'never any trouble, leastways none she can't handle.' I need her on my side or I'm in deep shit so to her surprise I ask her to take the register for me. The others sit in respectful silence while she belts out their names.

It's time for the bees to work their magic but already I can see the class in distinct groups. There are those who are noisy but who will also get on with the work and, what's more, do a really good job, then there are those who are noisy and will attempt the work in nibble-size bites to a generally decent standard, and there are those who are noisy and idle to the core. A lot of them seem really angry, really pissed off with everything to do with school and I feel like saying to them, 'hey kids, I'm not the enemy. I'm trying to help you.'

The clever gobby ones are the ones I like best. They have this real tough shell but inside there is natural talent. Some of these kids have the intellect, creativity, fortitude and resilience to make real and positive advances. Unfortunately, many are being lost through inadequate opportunities when they should be advancing to positions of power and influence.

One of the major obstacles for these kids is that their education takes place in an environment where as many as a third of their peers are disruptive. It's like trying to swim against a strong current wearing a diving suit. The disruptive element turn every lesson into a rodeo where I am the broncobuster. Unlike the wild west, the mustangs are never broken and I have to bust the same ones in every lesson. They kick and buck and twist and turn until eventually, towards the end of the lesson, they are frothing, panting and exhausted, but they are ready to be ridden, but when I get home on Friday every sinew in my body is aching.

```
Date: The Weekend
Location: Home
Enemy: Uncle Vanya
```

Sometimes I wonder what Friday nights would be like if I hadn't been 'busting the face' all week. Perhaps you need to visit hell in order to fully appreciate heaven. Six o'clock Friday evening, a nirvanic feeling that is already fading faster than the smoke in the St. Boswells kipper box. Yet, while it remains, everything is possible and Monday morning is a million miles away. I could go out tonight and do serious damage to myself and not have to rise in the morning. There were times when I used to do just that, but that was before weekends became finite. Instead, Margaret and I go to see Chekov's *Uncle Vanya*. The eponymous hero is the same age as me and it's dispiriting to see him portrayed as a wretched, cantankerous, alcoholic, lecherous loser. Chekov's characters are all looking for something, either from the past or the future, which is the root cause of most of their unhappiness. The play ends with Sonia repeating the mantra that, 'one day we will rest.' The revelation is cruel, they have played it by the rules and have achieved nothing, they have been cheated, there is no justice. The resonance is uncomfortable.

Date: Monday, 18.12.06
Location: Ellsworth   Primary,
somewhere in Mordor
Today's Enemy: Cars

7.30am. The phone rings. Will I go and teach a Year 6 class at Ellsworth Primary? Ellsworth has an evil reputation; I have heard that some of the kids there have long black pointy tongues, heads that turn 360 degrees and mothers that sell frocks in Hull. I want to shout 'No!' but my policy is to never turn work down - in the same way that a cork bobbing on the ocean has no say in which direction the currents take it, so I hear myself say 'yes,' for who am I to push against fate? The reason I am hesitant is purely through reputation. I recently swapped stories with a fellow supply teacher. It was like the meeting of two mercenaries, each trying to get one up on the other. 'Ah, but you should have been in Rwanda.'

'Rwanda? That was nothing. Have you been to Ellsworth?'

The stories have grown in stature until the school has gained an almost mythological status. There are some who even deny its existence. It is a kind of anti-El Dorado, the Mordor of all primary schools. There are tales of teachers going in as strong, virile, young happy men and women and emerging as insane, white haired, toothless crones. 'Yes, I will go. Year 6, you say.' I will take a cloak of invisibility, a shield, a couple of ham sandwiches and a pair of winged sandals.

Like most people, for years I have tried to get organised on Sunday evenings just to take the edge of Monday mornings, even if it is only to pre-pack my lunch, but I can't do it. Sunday is mine, it belongs to me, get your thieving hands off, it's all mine. As a consequence of this pathetic immaturity, Monday morning means throwing a bag of work together, making pack-ups, getting the kids school uniforms unravelled, writing cheques, ironing, showering, making breakfast, answering the phone, shaving, toileting and coffee making. At least I don't smoke anymore as I used to have fit three cigarettes in, too.

Monday morning. Outside the rain is hosing down and the wind is whipping up a soufflé of frenzy. It's disgustingly bleak and a long way from Honolulu.

For weeks, I have had this ongoing argument with my eldest son now in his first year at secondary school. He refuses to wear his coat and to make sure he doesn't have to wear it, he leaves it at school, for it is not cool to wear coats even when the weather conditions are extreme Arctic. The clock is ticking. I am tempted to cut two holes in a bin bag and make him wear that with a sign around his neck that reads 'How cool is this?' He looks at me with his shirt tail hanging out and his tie draped round his neck like a dead snake and I think *shit he's only twelve and he's got mid teen angst.*

I tell him to give me a break and that I am not the enemy and he mutters that I am the enemy and I ask him what he said and he says 'nothing' and I feel my blood pressure rising and I'm not even out of the sodding house yet. Meanwhile, his younger brother, still in Year 5, is snugly awaiting the outcome of this latest struggle in his new puffa jacket and hat. I give the eldest my cagoule to wear which trails down to his ankles. He observes my eyeballs rolling into the back of my head and accepts that all resistance is futile. I kiss him and off he goes. No doubt, it will be bagged as soon as he is out of sight and he will arrive at school looking like a cool drowned rat with pneumonia.

The words 'you are the enemy' whizz round the circle of death that is my skull as I start the car. The turning of the ignition only produces an ugly whining sound, the technological equivalent of a sick note. I don't have time to open the bonnet and blink inanely at the workings of an engine, so I rush to the bike shed. Bastard. The tyres are flat. I find the pump and blast air into them. The old ticker is racing now as the tyres inflate in a neat exchange of energy between man and machine. I saddle up and break out of the back gate into the alley like Batman out of his cave, admittedly more Adam West than Christian Bale these days, but still...

I whiz down the one-way streets the wrong way and blast a short cut through the park, through red lights and green men and down into the east end of town and into the surrounding estate of the notorious Ellsworth. Ahead, two rows of black grey council houses form a rotting tooth gauntlet and my bike rears up at the prospect. Down the centre is an enlightened councillor's vision of a green and pleasant land, but the thick black oozing sticky muddy strip and the burnt-out shells of cars are more evocative of the Somme. At the end of this dark passage lies Ellsworth. It is 8.40, I have five minutes. I twist the handlebars hard and stare into the distance, I feel the bike quiver beneath me but she holds steady as, head down against the lashing rain and wind, I press into the maelstrom and into the heart of darkness. At last I ride through the gates, my arrival unheralded, I lock up the bike (very securely, as it is my only means of escape) and realise that I have enjoyed the exhilaration of cycling with the wind in my hair.

I enter the domain and at once I am in a splendid hall of colour where the biggest and most beautiful Christmas tree I have ever seen greets me. The lights are on and the base is surrounded with candles and the children are arriving for assembly, all smartly dressed in pale blue tops complete with logo, which is not of a fire-breathing dragon chewing on a helpless maiden.

'I've done the register for you.'

A woman with a dark perm is smiling. 'I'm the new Head. If you want to go and have a cup of tea and settle in that will be fine.'

I do and I notice the pictures and the work on the walls and the displays and the time and energy that has been put into making this school an oasis in a troubled spot. This area does have problems, this is social worker city, but for a portion of every day, regardless of what shit is happening at home, the kids can see and understand that life isn't all misery and violence. This is not to say that all of the kids at the school have tough home lives, the vast majority live in good loving environments, but the area does have its fair share of problems and that's the simple truth.

The class returns from assembly, sits down and opens their reading books, presumably awaiting instructions and I am impressed to the point where I feel a pulse of excitement because I realise that here is an opportunity to have a really good productive learning and fun day with everyone working together. I spend the first lesson asking them about their interests and hobbies. There are several dancers whose routines sound gruelling, there is a boy who is a brown belt in karate, which is going some for a ten-year-old, and there is a boy who tells me that he is into weight training like his dad but he adds, 'my dad doesn't do it anymore because he fell off a cliff and broke his back.' Later, I meet their regular teacher and tell her what the kids have been telling me about themselves. She looks amazed and says, at regular intervals, 'really, I didn't know that.' During break, I talk to another supply teacher, a neat looking woman in her mid fifties with masses of grey hair tied up at the back in a loose bun. She has a vivacious personality and tells me that she is recently back from the jungles of Borneo where she lived for six weeks doing voluntarily work on a scientific research project. When she leaves, I surreptitiously touch the hem of her coat in the hope that some of her lust for life will rub off on me.

After break, I go for a high-octane lesson. It requires loads of energy but the results can be worth it. I tell them we are going to write some class poems and that everyone must have an input. The subject is colours and I write 'yellow' on the board saying, 'yellow is...' It's a brain storming exercise, tapping into a neuro-centre of spontaneity. The suggestions start to arrive, first as a trickle and then a nice steady flow until eventually we have:

<u>Yellow</u>
Yellow is a melon on a sunny day.
Yellow is a daffodil swaying in May.
Yellow is a lemon tangy and sour.
Yellow is a flower getting bigger by the hour.
Yellow is butter melting in a bun.
Yellow is corn growing in the sun.

<u>Green</u>
Is grass swaying on the ground.
Green is the grape ripe and round
Green is a scaly crocodile
Green is a lizard swimming in the Nile
Green is a bowl of mushy peas
Green is a hanky after a sneeze.

<u>Red</u>
Red is a massive rose
The shine on Rudolph's nose
A pair of big sisters night time lips
An apple full of pips
A cherry juicy and sweet
The beetroot that you eat.

A pair of big sister's night time lips. Fantastic.

At lunchtime I saw their regular teacher again and told her that the kids in her class were brilliant at poetry and once again, she looked puzzled.

'We don't do a lot of poetry,' she said. 'There isn't time.'

A few years ago, primary schools were defined by their individuality, as were the teachers who worked in them. When I was ten I had a teacher who was into history and, in particular,

Greek mythology. She was also a mean piano player who would play as we worked whenever the mood took her. Her music used to turn me into pink icing and at the end of the piece she would say, 'that was called the 'Trout' by Schubert.' We didn't do a lot on fractions that year, but we did get a classical education.

Five minutes to go until the end of school and I'm wondering just when the six headed dog of Ellsworth is going to make its appearance because so far I've seen nothing that fits the awesome reputation this school has gained. I've certainly had tougher assignments.

I still remember my tour of duty in Bradford - usually, waking up with a cinematic scream in the middle of the night, covered with a sheen of sweat. But when I received the call, my ethos then (as it is now) was that an ocean refuses no river and so I was up and away.

At 8.20am, I realised I was in trouble. It was rush hour and I didn't have a clue how to find the school. I had fifteen minutes before the school cancelled me and as I had been driving for nearly two hours to get there I could not let that happen. I pulled into the road side and looked at the address of the school and then at the A-Z but I couldn't concentrate due to the roar of intimidating 14 ton trucks that rolled by like small planets. Eventually, the A-Z transmogrified into a Mondrean painting. I was beat, the mission would have to be aborted unless a miracle occurred. It was then that I saw a sign pointing to the railway station. I was saved: where there are stations there are taxis. I drove up to the first in the rank with a shout of 'Hey cab. I'll follow you,' and off we zipped with the Asian driver periodically glancing at the address and in the rear-view mirror at me trying to follow him through handbrake turns and narrow streets until some twelve minutes later he pulled up outside the school. 'Three pounds,' he said and I thanked him because he had saved me a day's wages.

I was even early enough to notice that the name of the school had several metal letters missing and that some of the ones that were still pinned to the wall had flipped upside down so that it looked like the school was called St. Hitler's. The staff room was lit by a dangling, shadeless forty-watt bulb and in the murky corner sat an emaciated man with sparse ginger hair, a scruffy wispy beard and a stained black T-shirt who seemed to be in a trance.

'Excuse me,' I asked, aware of disturbing his reverie. 'But do you know where I can find the Headmaster?'

He looked up slowly and said, 'I am the Headmaster but I cannot deal with anything at present.'

Or perhaps he said, 'I cannot deal with the present.'

At that, he turned his gaze away again to indicate the brief audience was over.

Classrooms range in size from the shoe box to the luxuriously spacious and well appointed, but this was one of the former. The windows were high and afforded light grudgingly. At nine o'clock the class entered and continued to enter until I thought it was a set up for some cruel Channel 4 programme. It was like packing turtles into crates ready for airfreight. I was convinced they were going out of one door and coming back in another, but eventually the stream dried up and the class of ten-year-olds, possibly forty in number, sat down and looked up at me for guidance and instruction so I handed them out a pile of comprehension books.

Ten minutes later, after reading the passage describing the life of an Inuit Eskimo, I asked a girl at the front for the answer to a question appertaining to it. The girl smiled and I was reminded of a princess from the Arabian nights, from her silk dress to her fine Asian features and almond eyes. I asked her name but there was no response. I assumed she was shy, so I pointed to her friend and asked, 'What do you think the answer might be?'

Again, just a smile and then a giggle from another princess.

'Asimba and Tassin don't speak English sir,' said a large Asian boy.

'What, nothing?' I said.

'No sir, they are sisters. They have not been in Bradford long.'

'Niassa doesn't speak English either, sir,' put in another girl, and she reeled off another ten names at speed causing much mirth in the process.

'Some of the boys don't speak good English either, sir,' said the large Asian boy. 'They are refugees.'

The back wall of the room started to move towards me.

'Can I ask you a question now, sir?'

I didn't have time to accept or reject the request before he asked it anyway.

'How much do you earn in a week?

Once again, he allowed no time for an answer before betting that he earned more during one Saturday morning on his father's market stall than I earned in a week. I didn't doubt it, but meanwhile I still had to get through the day with forty kids, half of which didn't speak English, or at least professed not to. Tricky one, but as a member of the Special Ace Service you are trained to think on your feet and it must be remembered that I had recently had training in the teaching of drama.

I concentrated on the class spokesperson and said it would be a good idea for the non-English speaking members of the class if we could act out roles and that I would be a customer at his stall.

'That will be good,' he grinned and before I could say more he was out of his seat and leading me by the elbow to his imaginary clothes stall on Bradford market.

'Do you have children, sir? Boys or girls, sir, or perhaps you have been blessed with both?' he asked.

'Boys.'

'Excellent, sir. How many fine sons do you have?'

'Two.'

'Handsome like their father, sir, and very much liking football.'

'Yes.' I chuckled, slightly embarrassed, 'well, at least yes for the football.'

'Manchester United, sir, number 7 shirt originals, sir, half the normal price. You can have two for the price of one.'

'Er...'

'And what about something for your beautiful lady sir, see here, finest silk underwear. It will make her very happy, sir, and when woman is happy then man is happy, sir. Am I right, sir?'

The little stall owner was good and if it had been a real situation I would have been well out of pocket as the only English word he didn't seem to understand was the word no, as in, 'no thanks, it is the wrong colour, size and price.' Could our education system really offer this young gentleman anything more? He would waste years studying poetry and symbolism and acting like a tree and solving quadratic equations when he was already set up with a job for life.

On the way back I considered the Headmaster, the poor bastard; shell shocked, a zombie, the living dead, an officer unwilling or unable to leave his post, someone who would be found one morning with his brains spilling out over the sticky staff room carpet, his stiff fingers clutching a Webly service revolver. I have seen many teachers go that way; it begins with the carrying of a sustaining hip flask, sipping regular nips of tipple throughout the day. When I was teaching full time, I often had newly qualified teachers literally crying on my shoulders. A whole generation who don't have the time or energy to meet a man or a woman. I once thought about opening an agency that would allow discreet sexual encounters between young members of the teaching profession as a way of ensuring that at least some normality was maintained and that they weren't reduced to smacking the pony and spanking the monkey night after night. That is, if they had anything left in their wrists after an evening of marking and planning.

The classic case of all work and no play was revealed last term. I was teaching in a matriarchy of a primary school where ovaries rule and I was the token male, a figure to show the boys that owning a set of testicles does not necessarily prevent them from becoming a teacher. Between glances over her narrow shoulders, one young woman told me that she lived sixty miles away (due to house affordability) and that in order to keep on top of the pressure she got up at 4.30am and was at her desk at 6.45.

I thought this was impressive, but unfortunately for her, the Deputy Head put her to shame. Her organisation is meticulous to the point of each child's freshly sharpened pencil. The first time I took her class, she stayed in the room with me, giving up the allotted time she had been given for preparation. I was intrigued to see her hovering around the class like a fat bee in a flower patch periodically landing and probing before taking off again and landing elsewhere. Was she gathering the sweet nectar of childhood to allay the aging process? What evil was this I had uncovered? No, she was erasing the slightest blips in the children's writing with a giant tube of Tippex.

I have to say that any kid fortunate to be in her class would have had one big education as she worked her mammaries off for them. Also, her wall displays were something else, there was poetry and art on the walls that you would swear had been done by Keats and Raphael. This then was the expected standard that the narrow-shouldered NQT was expected to match and exceed. Most nights, she got home for 8pm and after a couple of hours marking, the rest of the day was hers to do with as she pleased.

I remember how pale and fragile she looked, like a figure from a Wilkie Collins novel. The hours were certainly Dickensian: I worked it out to be 18 a day. She would be too tired to even smack her pony. She was suffering. She was not happy and I felt that no matter how much she wanted to teach, she would be physically and mentally unable to keep up this gargantuan workload. She would crack and within three years would be forced out of the profession by an oppressive regime just like sixty per cent of all new entrants, adding to a deepening crisis, one that the government hopes to rectify with a bowdlerised D.H. Lawrence quotation ('Those who can - teach') and a six thousand pound bribe.

Perhaps this young NQT has been fooled into thinking she is earning good money, but 18 hour days dilute her pay to £1.60 an hour. Things must change for new recruits, or else we may have to return to conscription to ensure our charges have a chance in life.

Date: Tuesday, 19.12.06
Location: Copernicus Grove
Today's Enemy: Computers

Experience teaches that one's meat is very much another's poison as far as schools go. There are many factors involved in how you get on at a particular school, not least your prevailing mood. If you feel like shit it will be difficult to view the school objectively, especially if you've heard it's grim. Somehow, you must rise above your preconceptions - even when the old teachers in the staff room are letting out audible sighs of distress and some can't stop yawning. These are classic escape mechanisms of self-induced sleep often observed in animals used for testing purposes. Eventually, a bright little squirrel of a man appears. He's about fifty-eight and has that spring in his step that says 'just two more years and I'll be out', the one that prison trustees have. He is an adept who has the secrets of the alchemist and can arrange cover for every class by consulting his charts. His task is to keep the ship afloat no matter what tempests are delivered.

I am to teach Information Technology until lunch. He thrusts a map in my hand and a bunch of keys and scurries off to melt another pot of tar. What I know about IT can be written on the back of a gnat's bollock, but I am a professional in the Special Ace Supply and about to come under enemy fire. I face a bank of computer screens wondering from which direction the first volley will come. On the table is a brief that reads, 'They all know what to do' and I smile wryly at the sentence of death.

To my right the door implodes and they charge in, maybe twenty five or thirty Year 9s who throw their bags and coats into

SAS: Supply Ace Special

a heap in the middle of the floor and take up positions behind the screens. Sixty eyes staring me down.

'I have in my hand a piece of paper.' The famous words of Neville Chamberlain as he held Hitler's 'Peace treaty.' 'You all know what to do,' I say, thrusting the brief upwards and outwards and, in the land of cloud cuckoo, that would be the end of my input. Back in Realsville, however, a dozen hands are waving in the air for attention.

'I've forgotten my password.'

'I can't log on.'

'I've lost my work.'

'Houston, we've got a frigging problem.'

Suddenly, in a blaze of lights, a Year 11 boy appears.

'Can I use a spare computer to finish my homework, please?'

'On one condition.'

He smiles and obliges and tends to the raised hands like Florence Techno Nightingale until, one by one, the hands descend. For a while the ward is at peace and any time a plaintive cry is heard, he is there with his candle and his dextrous fingers and soothing knowledge. Mercifully, he stays all morning and I thank him.

'Sorted,' he says with a grin, clearly enjoying his newfound status. I think someone even called him Sir.

Lunchtime and this Special Ace Supply flight is due for a mid-air refuelling. Close by is a DIY store, so rather than sit and sigh in the staff room, I wander down the aisles of power tools and paint. I'll do anything rather than stagnate in a staff room. If there was a sewerage works nearby I would go there and watch the effluent being distilled into something pure. That would give me hope for some of my tougher classes.

Today I am happy to wander around the patio furniture, examining the crisscross trellis and dreaming of warmer days that must surely come. By aisle ten, I am feeling quite spiritual and begin to understand why DIY emporiums are the new cathedrals and why throngs of converts worship daily and why whole families turn out on Sunday. Louvre doors and garden decking, tiling grout and varnish, hardware, shelving, lighting, iron gates all the way to heaven. Over the past few years, I have done my share of DIY. I put it down to a mid-life existentialist crisis, connected with a marriage break-up, and an increasing feeling of becoming invisible. DIY was a method of proving to myself that I did actually exist, because if I didn't exist, then how come there is a shelf on that wall today, when there wasn't one there yesterday? And when is a shelf a shelf and not just a plank? What is the human equivalent of a plank becoming a shelf? Ah, so many questions…

Back to it. The second half. I managed to get through the first one unscathed. Just the afternoon now and that's it, land the plane and away. First, Geography with Year 10. The work is set. A few girls arrive first, all hair and lips; they sit petulant, chewing gum and screeching between utterances. It's going to be a tough one. Five hounds appear next; the lead one swings his bag like a gaucho's bolas as he enters. His chums follow, whooping and yelling like renegade Sioux Indians in a John Ford movie. Shit, I don't even have a white handkerchief, never mind a lance.

The lead hound barks loudest and the squaws seem to appreciate his demonstration of testosterone and bravado in the face of the taciturn General of the Seventh Cavalry. In situations like this, I have to make a choice between sitting back and letting them win, or making a stand. If I let them win, I can avoid a major confrontation. They will spend the lesson spiralling into a whirlpool of depravity and I will have added another layer of fur to my arteries. I will also lose self-respect, professional pride, dignity and self-esteem. I can't let this happen so it's a potentially lethal confrontation with the head honcho. His bag is swinging and whirling above the heads of the girls like helicopter rotor blades and I use my first tactic, and shout loudly. I once had singing lessons and know how to use the diaphragm for delivery.

No effect, so I move towards him and grab the bag, taking it clean. He approaches me and stands inches from my face. Christ, he's big, and he reeks of smoke. I see the poor condition of his skin, the violent eruptions around his lips and his dilated pupils. His warriors slip in beside him, smaller, skinnier, baring their sharp little yellow teeth, letting out the odd whoop to keep the pot simmering. I tell him he's going outside. He laughs but I'm not giving in. I tell him again and I hear the firmness in my voice, perhaps he does too. I have to be strong now because I am dealing with an unpredictable, drug-addled youth and panic could result in a really bad situation. I watch for a knife or any sudden movement that could indicate the onset of an attack. Red alert, red alert, adrenalin pumping, fight or flight, ready for action. *My piss is the strongest,* I keep telling myself, *my piss is the strongest*, until eventually they smell it too and they back off like a coven of hissing vampires from two rulers formed into the shape of a rudimentary cross. The girls have taken on a submissive posture and we can start the lesson.

Unfortunately, the hounds are not finished. They bang on the door and kick the wall until I am forced to confront them again. This time I go for assistance, but when I look through the window of the neighbouring class I see half a dozen kids standing on the tables having a full blown fist fight. I continue my search until I find an established teacher who orders them to the Head's office. Ten minutes later, they are back and kicking down the door. The cavalry have let me down again and so I battle out the final twenty minutes single-handed. I was all but scalped after that skirmish but the day wasn't over yet. I still had another double lesson to go: one hour ten minutes of it, four thousand eight hundred seconds, with a Year 11 bottom set. I pray that it will be a smoother ride, but as they leap into the classroom wielding tomahawks of abuse I lunge for the door, firing from the hip and only just make it to my big white horse. Hi ho, Silver! And away!

```
Date: Wednesday, 20.12.06
Location: Cherry Grove, somewhere
 South of paradise
Today's Enemy: Metal Stool Legs
```

Called into Cherry Grove High again. Cherry Grove the school of portacabins, Gormanghast kitchens, transparent panty lines and ecumenical matters. I'm teaching science today, so they supply me with a white coat with two pens in the top pocket and hey! I am a science teacher. I fluff up my hair and loosen my tie to go for the complete nutty scientist look and affect a Teutonic accent and a couple of nervous ticks to go for the big one, the megalomaniac going for world domination through means of my latest deadly invention.

The first lesson with Year 8 involves holding a test tube of soda water over a Bunsen burner until all the carbon dioxide has bubbled out of it, or 'effervesced' as they say in the trade. (See, the white coat does impart me scientific knowledge. Perhaps I have learnt it through osmosis.) I have been briefed by an unassuming lab technician called Jane who also works as a barmaid in the evenings. She chews gum and has an accent you could cut a steel hawser with but her organisation is empirically precise. In ten minutes I am kitted out with every piece of apparatus I will need for the day, from a rubber bung to a book called *Ten Basic Experiments,* which she probably wrote.

The world is full of Janes, the great-unacknowledged whose native intelligence and cunning ensure that idiots like me can bluff our way through the day. They are in every profession and are essential to the running of the entire system.

We need more Janes involved in running the country.

The lab is glacially cold but Jane advises me to get the Bunsen burners going. I remember them well and soon a dozen bright blue flames are bravely attempting to get the heat above freezing point before the class arrive. By the time they get here the temperature is industrially acceptable and we are ready to begin, and then my inner ear is violently assaulted by the sound of one hundred and fifty metal stool legs scraping across the floor as the kids sit down. The noise is excruciating, like a thousand finger nails scratching down a blackboard the length of Britain.

This is typical of the conditions in schools. In fact, it just about sums up all that is wrong in them. Their usual teacher must be suffering this aural torment every lesson and he probably doesn't know why he has to have the television on full volume and keeps saying 'sorry' when he is addressed. It's a health and safety issue that would not be tolerated in the private sector: their unions wouldn't allow it, whereas the teaching unions (an oxymoron if ever I heard one) won't even amalgamate. The solution to the chair problem is simple and costs sod all - put rubbers on the stool legs. Chair rubbers! You mad fool, you're a genius.

With one eye on the notes and the other on the bubbling test tube, I add a drop of litmus test and the water turns red.

'What does this mean?' I ask.

'It's acid.'

'Yes, but look what's happening.'

'It's turning yellow!'

'Yes.'

I'm just as amazed as they are.

'The liquid is turning neutral,' I declare, glancing at the textbook. 'This is because carbon dioxide is only soluble in cold water but not in warm.'

'What does soluble mean, sir?'

'Have you ever seen aspirins put in the water?'

'Yes. Our usual teacher does that all the time.'

'Right, and what happens to them?'
'They dissolve.'
'Exactly, they are soluble and so the colder the liquid, the more soluble the gas.'

Ok, it wasn't rocket science but it's one giant leap for me. Did I feel that I was cheating the kids by not being a genuine science teacher? No, because I gave it my best shot and didn't pretend to know anymore than I did. Plus, I had the coat.

The next lesson was taken by a student and I was there just for mere legal reasons. She was young, pretty and blonde with a body that had seen a lot of sweaty gyms. She wore a crop top that stretched over her breasts and rode above her flat toffee coloured tummy and I couldn't help but contrast her to Pickton, the wizened malevolent hunchback dwarf that taught me Physics. Young people like her are in short supply. Staff rooms are becoming increasingly full of the grey and the grizzled, only just falling short of handing out knee blankets and having a 32 inch TV on full blast. She was impressive, and if she was nervous, she didn't show it. The term 'no nonsense' was coined for her. She was an inspiration and you could see that the kids liked and respected her. I hoped that somehow she would stay in the profession for more than the statistical three years because to constantly lose highly trained people of her calibre is a social tragedy.

The final periods were with two lower sets. The first group were learning about the solar system and their task was to pick a planet to write about. The class in general seemed to be enjoying the task, apart from one boy who preferred to flick pellets.

'Shouldn't you be writing your project?' I asked.
'I don't know which planet I'm on,' he replied.
I didn't say anything.

Date: Christmas
Location: Log fire
Enemy: Commercialism

Ah, carol singers.
'We wish you a merry Christmas and a happy new year.' That was it. No more, followed by a sharp rap on the door. No preceding carols and even the begrudged yuletide greeting abridged. I'm surprised they don't just kick the door in and menacingly demand a fiver.

Teachers really come alive during their holidays. For the rest of the time they are like vampires in caskets waiting for the night. Holidays are what the job is all about: freedom from the daily cosh. Christmas, Easter and summer: the holy trinity. There has been talk of abolishing the summer holiday but any government that implements that would bring the world of education crashing down. The summer holiday is sacrosanct, if anything it is too short: leave well alone. Christmas is ritualism and I don't care.

I loved watching my youngest son play the witch in the school pantomime and basked in both sons decorating the tree as they have done since they could stand. I like to see the ornaments appear for yet another year. Some are over forty years old now and once dangled on my mother's tree. I like the fires and the fairy lights and *The Snowman*, even the bit at the end when he rushes out to play with his new friend only to find him melted in the sun with just a pathetic hat and scarf left as a reminder. It's devastating, and that's before that heart breaking violin cuts in. Christmas isn't easy when you are separated and you have children so the past few years have seen me going to their mum's house to open presents and then returning home at lunch time. They go for a big turkey dinner with traditional trimmings dinner at a friends house and as Margaret is a vegetarian we have a piece of lettuce and a bag of cashew nuts. Not really, Margaret makes a superb three course vegetarian meal, and I don't miss the ritual of chewing on a cardboard box at all.

SAS: Supply Ace Special

Date: Monday, 15.01.07
Location: Elmsfare Wood, very far from New Zealand
Today's Enemy: Mums

A twenty-mile drive which is a bind. The tailbacks on the highway are so long that I drive in first gear for a journey that should take twenty minutes but now takes an hour and a half. The worst thing is the bastards who have the chutzpah to leave it to the last minute before edging into the queue after us poor suckers have patiently waited our turn. It happened again this morning. Someone cut in front of me at the last minute so I pressed the horn for a full five minutes and flashed my lights until I felt the rubber bands tighten around my chest. I forced myself to calm down then for fear of having a massive attack. What a bum way to go: a corpse in a car on a cold grey day, stiffening in a traffic jam.

I first taught at this school last year after being sent there by an agency. At the end of the school day the Headmistress said she would prefer to phone me direct: it's cheaper that way and I get a contribution to my pension from the county. I am their chief supply now. Since I've been coming here, they have lost two brilliant young teachers. One is a young woman who now sends e-mails from New Zealand where she is white water rafting, horse riding and 'blokeing' with her twin sister (another ex-teacher.) Well done girls, you made it, you took the great leap.

The other ex-teacher is a young man who has opened a café in Cornwall with his partner (yet another ex-teacher.) He has been back to visit since and is reported to look fifteen years younger.

This is good going, as he was only twenty-five when he left.

The kids here are polite, helpful and pleasant. Here it is possible to periodically take my foot off the gas. I can liken a typical day at some schools to driving on a motorway with the accelerator jammed at ninety. Over the weekend, I record tapes of Radio 4 programmes to help me over the boredom of traffic jams. This morning I listened to *The Jimi Hendrix Story* and was duly distracted from crushing reality by stories of Eric Clapton sitting in the dressing room, head in his hands, having agreed to let Hendrix support his band The Cream.

In the past, I have attempted to learn French, German and Spanish from cassettes. The cod French accent and the unnecessary accordion music did for that language. The fact that my car was stolen, complete with the German course, did for that language, and the Spanish teacher's harsh inquisitional voice tone did for the Spanish. Usually, I just dip into my carrier bag of ancient tapes. I love music, all types, I used to know every band on *Top of the Pops* but somewhere around the early eighties, I lost touch. Bands like Hazy Fantazy caused an abrupt end of interest.

I remember watching *A Clockwork Orange* in my early teens and seeing the listed top ten as Alex wandered through a futuristic record shop. I didn't recognise any of the bands and to me this was as inconceivable as becoming a teacher. Somewhere in the eighties, the unthinkable happened on both counts, I no longer recognised the top ten and I became a teacher after taking a psychology degree in London, having a stint as a milkman on the Isle of Dogs and enduring a PGCE at York.

I maintain a low-key presence in this school even though the staff know me well enough. The Head likes me because I avoid the staff room. Headteachers do not like garrulous outsiders or serpents whispering dissatisfaction.

Today, I'm in charge of 28 six-year-olds.

'The Head says you like to do your own thing,' says the young Geordie woman. She looks a whiter shade of pale and is a long way from 'blokeing it' in New Zealand.

'I don't mind a few pointers in the right direction,' I tell her.

She uncoils several scrolls of papyrus covered in a fine print, almost invisible to the naked eye; her lesson plans for the day.

'I hope these are passable,' she smiles.

I reduce her reams of instruction to three key words for each lesson. It is not done through arrogance, just practical necessity. 9.00am and all the little people enter. Their mums come too, all sizes, shapes, colours and neuroses from chain-smoker thin to tracky-bottomed fat. I always feel uncomfortable with the mums about because I can almost hear them thinking, 'what the hell is a man doing here? He must be gay. Why isn't he on a building sight or anyplace that requires the wearing of a hard hat?'

The situation isn't helped when one little girl clutches her mother's coat and shrieks like a split bagpipe at the prospect of being left with the ogre who will surely eat her, pigtails and all. The mother is a rosy-cheeked blonde who is becoming rosier by the second as she tries to prise her child's head out from under her jumper.

'Can't you take Olivia off me?' She pleads.

I advise 'Rosie' to take her child to the Headmistress until she settles down as I am more frightened of her than she is of me. After all, she's the one who looks like a vampire with her missing front teeth and big canines.

Meanwhile, the rest of the class are sitting on the carpet, licking their lips and thinking that this could be interesting. The stricken Olivia is later brought in by the Headmistress like a babe in arms and sits guzzling her thumb while I take the register. Registers can provide much entertainment due to my mispronunciation of the children's names, 'it's Kylie,' I am informed with a heap of giggles, 'not Kayleigh.' Then there is the 'Bond' boy called James who understandably and instantly demands that he is called Jamie, the 'Horner' boy (called Jack) who I later had to send to a corner for being naughty, a girl called Bacardi, another called Ikea (which actually sounds quite nice) and, strangest of all, a little plump kid with round National Health Service spectacles called Wyatt Earp. I am not making this up.

By the end of the register, Olivia has calmed down. I have been here a whole ten minutes and as far as she can see all the children appear to have their arms and legs still attached. By lunchtime, she is happier than a baby hippo in a mud hole and is grinning in gap toothed pleasure at George the green guitar.

I call him that to any class under Year 4. If I called the guitar George to Year 6, they would mentally toss me into a room marked very uncool and throw away the key. Young children adhere to the idea of my guitar being a free thinking spirit who has the ability to even talk and, best of all from my point of view, to have mood swings, because if they are too noisy then there is no way that George will come out of his box. It works. When George is emerging from the guitar case you can hear the ruffle of a kangaroo's fur somewhere out in Bunga Bunga. So we sing a few songs and everyone is happy, especially Olivia who laughs likes a pig at the silly old ogre.

Lunchtime and the kids have been brilliant, which is fortunate as there is never any support. It's just me and thirty effervescent six-year-olds. Is it too much to ask for another pair of hands? Is there not a fat-arsed mother out there somewhere who could give up one afternoon of Oprah, even if it's just to help with shoe lace tying? No point complaining though, one Special Ace Supply motto is, *del mundis et gratio lucet nuncio* - 'Expect nothing. You will not be disappointed.'

The lesson after lunch is entitled 'The Titanic.' A topic they are experts on due to the movie. I am mightily impressed by their knowledge and we spend the afternoon making paper ships courtesy of the little bit of origami that I have developed over the years. The result is a success rate of eighty percent, which amazingly never fluctuates whatever the age group. When they finish the ship they get to colour it in, then they glue it to a sheet of A3 and create a background where the only limitation is their imagination. I recall one kid placing his ship on the pock-marked surface of the moon with a background of black and gold stars and a far distant earth. I wonder what he's doing now.

3.30pm and the mothers start appearing outside of the windows, just one at first, then a pair, then a few more, arriving like the birds in Hitchcock's eponymous film. A few more now, pecking at the windows. I like to finish with a song in primary schools, usually it's *Twist Again*. I tell them that the best twisters get to leave first. 'Come on, let's twist again,' I sing and they are off, twisting like crazy and laughing out loud and Olivia is there, knees bent and hands on hips, tossing her ringlets from side to side like some heavy metal head banger half way through the screaming guitar solo of *Ace Of Spades* while her mother peeps through the window and wonders what happened to the weepy little introvert she dragged squealing into the classroom only this morning.

Date: Tuesday, 16.01.07
Location: Whiteside, deep in the trenches
Today's Enemy: Grey Wire, Black Teeth and Blue Boys

A few months ago I was called into a tough primary school (sadly, no oxymoron.) It was a place where your regular supply teachers fear to tread, but as I am a member of the elite Special Ace Supply and the proud holder of a canary yellow beret, I accepted at once. I was greeted in the car park by a grey haired, red faced, wiry man who passed comment on the beamer, it was neither negative or positive but simply, 'big car.' I later found out that he was the acting Headmaster, the usual one and his deputy were both down with stress. Not unusual, they often go down in pairs as the result of too much late night planning, the consequent mulling over of life's vagaries and the desperate need to escape.

The Year 5 class I was asked to teach were, in his words, 'a right nasty set of vindictive little buggers.' I was soon to find out just how true this was: that day, I used all my aces (and both jokers) to keep a lid on them.

'Well done,' said the grey wiry Head, 'not many come out on top with that class but they seem to have enjoyed you.' I always find that phrase interesting, 'the class enjoyed you.' It makes you out to be no more than a tasty morscl thrown to a crocodile or a curtain raiser in a gladiatorial contest, which is more than apt. 'Could you come back tomorrow?'

My first instinct was to laugh loud and hysterically but as the following day was Friday followed by Dr. Weekend I said yes. I knew there was trouble ahead though as the Head phoned me up at home that evening to ask if I had punched a boy earlier that day. Once more, my first instinct was to laugh hysterically, but I realised that this could quickly turn sour. I could have told him that I wouldn't be coming in the next day but I felt as though that would be admitting guilt.

The following morning I was asked to meet with the Headmaster, the boy and the boy's mother in his office. The mother was positively medieval, a twenty stone horror in leggings, stumpy black teeth complete with a bean-stained sail size T-shirt. I insist I'm not being cruel here, but if her boy had been a piglet and she was a sow she would have rolled over him at birth.

As it was, here he was now, all three stone of him accusing all six feet four of me of punching him on the arm. Common sense would decree that if a very big man punches a skinny little kid on the arm, then there will be evidence of such an action in the form of a bruise as black as his mum's incisors, but no, nothing: not even a hint of canary yellow. Still the crazy cow was adamant that her darling had been punched.

Now come on, how long would I last as a supply teacher if I was going round schools duffing up kids? Yet the more I denied it, the more guilty I seemed to become until in the end the Headmaster took me aside and said, 'Be honest now. Did you punch him?' Amazing! It was like good cop, bad cop. 'We have a witness,' he went on.

'A witness?'

'Yes, his friend says you punched him.'

'His friend?'

'Yes.'

'Ok,' I said, 'let's hear the witness but first of all, before he comes in, let's ask the victim just exactly whereabouts I punched him.'

The grey wire agreed.

'Right, young man,' said Grey Wire, 'where exactly did the teacher punch you?'

'There, right there, hard,' said the boy, rubbing the bicep of his right arm.

'Are you absolutely sure?'

'My boy doesn't tell lies,' hissed the mother.

'We'll now bring in Liam,' said Grey Wire, 'and ask him what he saw.'

Both mother and son looked smug as a boy of ten (going on thirty) strolled into the room like a condensed version of Vinnie Jones.

'You understand how serious this is now, don't you?' Said Grey Wire, 'you must tell the truth.'

The little bulldog nodded.

'Whereabouts exactly did you see the teacher punch your friend?'

'Here,' said the eye witness, pointing to his stomach, 'he was punched right hard just there, wasn't you?'

The victim simultaneously looked bewildered, petrified and furious.

'Are you sure it was the stomach, nowhere else?'

'Yes,' said the little white bull, 'he smacked him hard right in't guts.'

At this point a normal mother would have apologised for her son's attempt to wreck some poor bastard's life, but not this special lady.

'You cheating bastards!' She screamed. 'I'll get even you clever cunt. Keep looking over your shoulder.'

At that she lifted her son bodily, steamed out of the room, and nearly flattened the baffled boy witness whose 'did I do good?' was cut off somewhere between larynx and tongue.

When the last of her echoing expletives had bounced down the stone steps of the austere Victorian school, Grey Wire smiled contritely and said, 'well, you still have a class to teach.'

Surprised, but not shocked, I told him that the risk factor was too high and that I would be the one to decide when my career was over not some malicious kid and his odious mother. To this day, I still have no idea why the boy made the accusation.

So today I was called to Whiteside, a first for me. I am greeted by the Headmaster…Shit! Grey Wire! He is covering for the usual Head who is off with 'long term illness.' Like true professionals, we don't mention 'the war' but I get the feeling that (even though I was exonerated) he still holds me responsible for screwing up his day all those months ago. All I want from today is for everything to run smoothly, but during registration one of the kids begins to cry and squeal like a leveret on national hare coursing day just as Grey Wire appears to inform me that I am to cover playground duty.

I hate duty, it's too bloody risky. The kids hurl themselves around like blood cells in a centrifuge while I pray that they don't collide. Not today. I feel the eyes of Grey Wire multiplying into a thousand kaleidoscopic images waiting, just waiting, for something to happen. To my left a group of Year 6 kids are forming a human pyramid, it doesn't look safe, if it collapses…shit, too late, three big fat girls bounce off the stricken form of a boy with a blue face, he isn't moving, I rush over and he's turning purple, he's not breathing, Christ he's choking and I'm surrounded by every kid in the school with the smaller ones scrambling on the back of the big ones to catch a glimpse of boy blue. I put him over my knee and thump him between the shoulder blades and he coughs out a 2p coin and splutters and cries and sucks in the air of life and as I look up there is old Grey Wire, bordering on apoplexy, bluer than the boy, with all his child-abusing suspicions confirmed.

'Jack were choking, Sir,' comes a voice from the back.
'He were nearly dead.'
'He were dead!'
'Sir brought him back to life, Sir.'
Grey Wire calms down, but only a little for as far he's concerned I am still guilty. I almost feel like apologising. Then

Grey Wire says, 'well, you've still got a class to teach.'

I felt like running for cover again but I'm glad I stayed because I experienced one of those rare and beautiful instances when I was actually in the present, not the future nor the past, but actually in the present. It happened during a PE lesson. I was taking no further risks, so I got the kids to lie on the floor and just relax while I played the piano. The sun streamed through the windows and lit up their faces and as I played with the sun on my back and listened to the music and followed my own instructions to breath deep I became part of the moment.

There were no further incidents until, on the way out, I found my car totally boxed in next to the ornamental border of the school garden. It was a tight fit but due to an overwhelming desire to just get the hell out of there I somehow managed. Only when I returned to base did I note that the car bonnet was covered in pine needles, tree bark and sweet smelling roses.

SAS: Supply Ace Special

Date: Wednesday, 17.01.07
Location: St. Boswells, sixth circle of hell
Today's Enemy: Unions

An unusual assignment. I was approached a couple of weeks ago by a member of the management at St. Boswells. It was at the end of a particularly harrowing hour trying to teach the usage of the semi-colon to 9X. The member of the senior management team was dressed sixties style, but without the flippity floppity hat. Her hair was bright red to match her unfeasibly long fingernails and she had more twitches than a shot cowboy in a Sam Peckinpah movie. In a series of lisps and rolling R's she asked if I would teach a fifteen-year-old boy who has been expelled. Often, these cases go against the wishes of the unions and the teachers at the school, so I'm not keen to get involved. She promised that it was not a union issue and that the boy was out of classes for his own development.

This morning I was introduced to the boy, Declan, and we got down to work in a large room complete with leather clad table and tea making facilities. Declan is built like the proverbial brick shithouse. He has a number one haircut, a plump face and big sad eyes which all club together to make him look like a baby seal, though a bloody dangerous one if crossed. He tells me that he's heavily into Rugby League and Union and that he plays for three clubs and the County and will soon to be on the books of Leeds Rhinos.

'I want to play for the British Lions. I train every night.'

The task today is to complete an English assignment. He is way behind having been expelled since March, almost a year ago. The brief is to find an advert in a magazine and to analyse the methods of persuasion it uses. We discuss it and Declan has some good ideas. Suddenly, as we sit around the leather table, drinking coffee and discussing the merits of an advert for Cadbury's mini chocolate fingers, we become advertising executives! By lunchtime, we have analysed the graphics, text, free offers, colours, font, caption, targeted sector, genre, context, the rule of three, and have drawn up a conclusion and a final evaluation. There are ten sides of notes and by the end of the afternoon, they have been typed and placed into a plastic folder ready to present to a prospective client. At three o'clock I feel strange because the usual adrenaline isn't pumping through my system and my face is not bright red.

It makes me realise just how damaging to your health teaching can be when the usual symptoms of tension and stress are seen as normal. Worse, the moral for pupils is - if you want a one to one education, disrupt your class and threaten to punch your teachers gum's out.

Date: Thursday, 18.01.07
Location: St. Boswells, near Baghdad
Today's Enemy: Odours

It's Thursday morning at St. Boswells and the Year 10 boys shuffle in. Billy is first. My first reaction is to scream, 'Christ Billy! You smell like a dead dog, you dirty little bastard, you're nearly sixteen and should be attracting women, not flies.' But I don't because he's a decent enough kid, he's just sloth idle like his peers in this set. Chris flaps in next, the usual inane yellow buck toothed grin on a plump white featureless face crowned with a few tufts of mangy black hair that gives him the look of a mutant coconut.

Chris is obsessed with an American beauty called Buffy. He reads all the books, watches the TV programmes and has a bedroom full of her posters. He shows me her picture in a magazine and I can see the attraction for a fifteen-year-old boy. If only she was a healthy cheerleader or a short order cook or a pre-med student instead of a vampire slayer. I have ten regulars in this class, there should be sixteen but the others take it in turns to appear in court. I quickly learned that to try and to get some traditional work out of these guys would be like trying to eat soup with chopsticks, so I bring in magazines such as *What Car?* and ask them to pick a car, draw it and write down a few features about it. It works well and there have been moments when the classroom has taken on the feel of a Ford design office. What's more, the work produced has been to a high standard and is now on the wall. There has been criticism, however, from another member of the English department who has informed them that their work 'is not English, but merely Art.'

At lunch time I go to the staff room. I have a bit of a chest virus and it's making me hot and tired and short of breath. Usually I skip this place because it's depressing but today at least it's warm and I lie across five black vinyl seats and fall asleep. There was a time when I would have been too embarrassed to fall asleep in a staff room but now it seems the sanest, most obvious thing to do because when I wake up I am refreshed and feel a little better in body, mind and soul. I look round at the tired faces in the staff room.

I don't think its tub-thumping to advocate that teaching is now a blue collar job and has been ever since the middle classes started jumping the badly holed ship. The idea of the middle and upper classes even considering teaching as an option is now implausible - they moved on years ago to the lush lands of accountancy, media, law and finance. Meanwhile, successive governments have continued to erode the status of teachers through low levels of pay, opportunities, and conditions.

Now, the choice of teacher as a career comes somewhere between cong scourer and muleskinner. Incidentally, a cong scourer is someone in the Middle Ages who scrubbed out the cesspits of the big houses. Plumbing was basic then and shit would drop from the garderobes into a bricked up building which, when full, was raked out by the said professionals. It was a family thing and they travelled from house to house underneath a black cloud of flies. Perhaps the reasons why teaching and state education as a whole has been allowed to slip to such unprecedented levels of impoverishment is because Government ministers send their kids to private schools and thus develop a nice pair of blinkers that close a little more every day to the point of tunnel vision. Also, whenever there is a visit, the true picture of the school is distorted by virtue of their political presence, just like when the Ofsted Stormtroopers appear. You could say the same for the health service, which is also on the way to becoming a blue collar job because the middle and upper class students are not that big on altruism anymore. It's hard work contributing to society, especially with all those TV channels, magazines, record companies and finance houses to work for.

The plus side of working at St. Boswells is that the afternoon consists of one double lesson and that's it, just land the plane and go home. On Thursday, I have a routine of driving from St. Boswells straight to Tescos where I have my tea. Afterwards, I do the shopping and then go to a sculpting class. If I went home first and went into couch potato mode I would become an obdurate force and my creative endeavours would start and finish at the 'oh, it's too dark, cold and wet' hurdles.

Like a lot of things in my life, the sculpting happened by chance. I was actually heading for a course entitled 'Stone carving for fun' in order to knock frustrated lumps out of a chunk of limestone. However, I followed the wrong crowd and ended up on a first level-sculpting course. I didn't discover that I was on the wrong course until two months later but by then I was making clay ears. The tutor is a thirty-year-old Albanian called Andrian who was recently called the 'new Michelangelo' in a *Times* article. He is a brilliant teacher because he lets you struggle until you bleed before demonstrating how to create an ear just like the one that poor Vincent lost, the one sticking to the side of my head, in fact, everyone's head, apart from the head of the cop in *Reservoir Dogs*.

```
Date: Friday, 19.01.07
Location: St Magdalenes, somewhere
 near Pluto
Today's Enemy: Ultramodernism
```

I'm always wary of schools named after the pious and holy as the reality never matches the intended connection. It is miles away too, on the other side of Leeds and too far out of my territory, but still I take it.

The school is ultramodern, being only two years old, and is built on a half wheel principle with the central hub containing the brain, and the spokes leading off to the different departments of molecular transformation, advanced robotics, astro-engineering, bio-mechanical information theory and woodwork. Being there was like borrowing American troops' equipment: suddenly, the SAS go from slingshots and mouldy cabbages to heat-seeking SCUD missiles.

The staff have plastic passes dangling from their necks as some sort of security device. The doors open with a card swipe and a swish. However, like HAL in *2001*, there are problems. Recently a domestic science teacher was forced to spend the night sleeping on one of her kitchen surfaces because the doors have a time lock. In St Magdalenes, no-one can hear you scream.

I am invited to sit outside the Deputy Head's office to await further instructions and every smart-arsed plastic dangler who walks past thinks it's a hoot to say, 'that's where the naughty boys sit.' Eventually, I was given my mission for the day, and I realised that all this gorgeous equipment came at a price: my timetable was full of bottom set Year 10s and 11s. On route to the first class I overheard a giant teenager ask his mate if he fancied 'legging it?'

'No way,' replied his ferrety pal, twitching his whiskers and rubbing his paws in anticipation, 'we've got a supply teacher.'

The lesson was Craft Design and Technology, which has come a long way since I left school with a pair of odd-legged callipers fashioned out of steel with my bare hands over a period of two years. One day I will use them for their intended purpose when I discover what that is. The task today is to make sketches for a bed design and, with all the enthusiasm of a group of teenagers that have been asked to design a bed, they reach interminably for their pencils. For the next hour there is monastic silence and even the occasional snore as they complete their preliminary drawings. At the end of the lesson I review their work and pass constructive comments on their efforts. Most are fairly prosaic but one girl has excelled with a four poster, pink and black, star shaped, sheepskin, water bed packed with must-haves like inbuilt speakers, a giant screen, a fridge for alcopops, a snack cupboard, an ashtray, mirrors on the canopy and air jets coming out of the mattress that allow her to 'float off to sleep.' The boys liked this one, it kind of caught their imagination and suddenly spotty ginger Gill is looking more of a proposition.

I spent lunchtime on the bridge of the *Enterprise*, a circular staff room with four different entrances all going swish as the plastic danglers arrived carrying their luncheon gamma pills. What amazes me is that they all wear their danglers with pride. I discerned also that there were different colours of dangler according to department. People love this. I remember when I was nineteen and working at Sellafield as a process worker. Everyone had to wear a hard hat. The electricians wore red, the instrument mechanics wore blue, the scientists wore green, the engineers wore orange, the management wore purple and we got to wear plain boring white. That is, until I sprayed all the helmets in our section with gold paint and received a written warning.

After lunch I am asked to do PE. This involves timing the Year 10 boys over 800 metres and categorising them into gold, silver and bronze levels according to their times. In the first group the race is won by a future Olympian, he streaks around the track in a time of one minute fifty eight seconds while the mortals stagger across the line up to three minutes later. In the fourth race a boy lines up who is the fattest kid I have ever seen and I am seriously concerned for his heart, but what can I say? 'Hey you, fatso don't even think about it, I don't want a death on my hands.'

Fortunately, he sets off at a pace in keeping with his size. Instead of the other boys giving him abuse for his size and lack of athleticism, they all join him for the last lap and move at his pace, encouraging his every lumbering step, and as he gets into the home straight they back off and yell encouragement as if he's about to take the Olympic title and break the three minute mile in the process, and the fat boy is going for it, he's picking up the pace as his face turns fire engine red and the screams behind him get louder and he goes for it and he's going to finish. It may have taken him nearly ten minutes but he's going over the line and the other boys whoop and rush over and mob him and the fat boy's face explodes into the most beautiful smile and Jesus Christ, I'm crying.

SAS: Supply Ace Special

```
Date: Weekend
Location: Home
Enemy: Time
```

The weekend. Where did it go?

```
Date: Monday, 22.01.07
Location: Hinton Valley, all along
  the A59
Today's Enemy: The Staff Room
```

I had no teaching booked today and was looking forward to having a day off. The golden minutes between 7.20 and 7.50 had been and gone. It was looking good but then a call came from a new agency. I was reluctant to accept because I had formulated plans for a pleasant day, just catching up on my life, but then I considered the cost of recent car repairs and found myself on the road to Hinton Valley village primary school. I arrived at 9.40 to teach a Year 5 class in a portacabin. The Head, a Jim Dale look-a-like, was covering. 'Carry on teaching,' whispered Jim. Assembly was at 10.15 but a fat bespectacled woman in a lilac fleece informed me that I didn't have to stay for it. Good. I took the opportunity to get my bearings and was aware of the surrounding fields. A run-down portacabin perhaps, but one that was floating on an ocean of green. Half finished bird boxes were at the back of the room and outside the window were nesting boxes on trees, alive with all varieties of tits and finches.

An hour of numeracy next with the top set and then lunch. The weather was grey but mild so I ambled into the village centre for a sausage and egg sandwich.

'Do you want any sauce?' Asked the Barbara Windsor look-a-like.

'No, missus no,' I replied in my best Frankie Howard voice.

Later, in the staff room, an eccentric woman full of strange hand and facial gestures (another frustrated thespian) shouted at

SAS: Supply Ace Special

me across the sticky grey carpet, 'I was in your part of the world recently, at a sing along *Sound Of Music*. The audience dress up, you know, *Rocky Horror* style, only more bizarrely, with grown men in lederhosen, SS uniforms, nuns (always dodgy) and goat herds (lonely ones.) You ought to go next time.'

I smiled.

'What do men supply teachers do on their days off anyway?' she asked, 'A woman would have lots of domestic chores to deal with whereas men…play golf, I suppose,' she said dreamily. I left quickly and chastised myself for entering that universal chamber of rocky horrors known as a staff room. Ah, what the hell, she was just being friendly.

The afternoon began with a video about the working conditions of navvies and housemaids during the Victorian era. The navvies seemed to be having a good time with their Irish drinking songs and fist fights despite the fact that on the Carlisle-Settle line alone over a thousand of them were killed and hundreds more maimed. The final session saw the kids going into different groups for project work, one of which involved simply staring out of the window at the nesting boxes. Brilliant!

**Date: Tuesday, 23.01.07
Location: Amber Woods, somewhere in the future
Today's Enemy: Switches**

I rise in the dark and count the switches I throw, fourteen including the light switches kettle, radio, central heating and shower switches. I am robot man. I am so programmed that at 6 am on Saturday and Sunday, my body is on full alert and I have to fight to stop my legs from getting out of bed. The kettle boils while I shower and shave underneath the warming waters. I drink strong coffee from a pint mug and make sandwiches. I eat toast on the hoof and listen to the stories of man's inhumanity to every living thing and the inane thought for the day on Radio Four, which always begins with a curved ball to get your interest ('Believing in God is like having a Thai massage...')

Later, I wake the boys and force them to acknowledge my existence by saying 'good morning Dad' through clenched teeth. On Wednesday mornings I drop them off at their Mum's house knowing I won't see them until the following Sunday. We've been doing this for four years now but it still makes me feel profoundly miserable as I drive off in the dark. Sometimes, I get angry too because I feel that precious time with them has been denied but mostly I just feel fortunate. Statistics say that two years after a divorce, the father is completely off the map. Last week their friend's dad left a note to say he was leaving to live with a woman in Germany. Amazing.

Six years ago Amber Woods School burnt down. It was an old Victorian building and it took five years to rebuild. In true phoenix fashion, the school has risen from the ashes and is now one of the most modern in the country. We are talking glass ceilings (or floors, depending where you're coming from) with designer furniture and advanced computer suites.

I arrive in time to study the 'flight plan' and it looks a good one. I am to discuss Victorian houses and architectural features. Most of the kids in this school live in houses just like these. I draw panelled doors, tiled floors, stained glass, sun lights, coving, ceiling roses, dado rails, picture rails and fireplaces complete with roaring flames. The class enter and are uncannily quiet but I remain alert because kids are kids whether they are from humble tumble down estates in Leeds or from splendid four up four down Victorian desirables. Listen to any playground in the country and you will hear the sounds of an urban jungle, a mixture of trill shrieks, snarls, screeches, squeaks, squeals, yells, howls, wailing, hollers, bays, bawls, cries, maniacal laughter, moans, yowls, keens, squalls and right in the centre of it all a terrifying, hair standing on end, glass shattering, primeval scream.

I remember teaching a class of seven-year-old angels who seconds after leaving the class room shouted, 'Paul Costa, you are a cunt...' Without guidance, children would make the African Savannah seem as tame as a happy clappy picnic. The class enjoy learning about the work on Victorian houses and are keen and enthusiastic when it comes to sketching them. None more so than the girl who points to her drawing and says, 'Where shall I put the dildo rail?'

```
Date: Wednesday, 24.01.07
Location: Amber Woods, somewhere
 in the future
Today's Enemy: Administration
```

Amber Woods again. A double. It could have been a treble, and what a pleasant week that would have been. It would have been like a holiday but I am committed to a regular slot at St. Boswells.

My brief today is to, 'Get them to design wallpaper in the style of William Morris.' That is some task when you consider it. I don't know a lot about wallpaper or William Morris, apart from the fact that his name was William Morris and he was famous for wallpaper. I like this part of the job though. Not many occupations provide the kind of variety that you can get as a primary school teacher, apart from stand up comedians who present TV and radio programmes on everything from hitchhiking with fridges to rebuilding steam engines.

It's the administration that kills the job, sure as a Russian vine will choke your prize roses. The constant evaluation is insulting to the intellect and professional integrity of teachers.

A few years ago, when I worked full time, I had a friend called James who taught PE. James used to give up his free periods to help a teacher who was heading for her third nervous breakdown in as many years. None of the kids in her class could read or write so James offered to read them a story at the end of the day. This resulted in the kids having a good laugh and leaving the premises feeling good, plus the poor female teacher was given a respite from the six hours of torture she endured every day. At this particular school there was an acting Head who thought only of his own career advancement. He and James did not get on. During yet another meeting on how to write lesson plans, he tried to use James as an example of how not to do it, but it backfired beautifully.

'If we look at what Mister O'Connell has written for the last lesson on Friday, it says 'Reading.' Reading what, Mr. O'Connell, *The Sun*?'

'*The Three Little Pigs*,' answered James.

'And what is the aim, target, goal and object of the lesson, Mr. O'Connell?'

'Simple,' said James, 'the target, goal and object is to tell the kids a traditional fairy story that they can relate to and which will give them the rudiments of story construction. Here we have three little pigs, where one is an incident, two is a pattern, and three breaks it. One tells us what the risk is; two confirms what wrong behaviour is and at three we know the rules and so can appreciate what the smart person needs to do in order to break the unsuccessful pattern and win.

'You see if the three little pigs was just one big pig that built a house of bricks in the first place, and the wolf couldn't get in, no matter how much he huffed and puffed, then we have conflict but no tension or drama. Anticlimax. No story. *Three Little Pigs* is suspense, pattern, and contrast, all in one little story and the aim is stop the kids climbing up the frigging walls for ten minutes.'

The staff laughed loud and actually cheered him. It was brilliant and after that the Head posed no threat to anyone.

There are several fine examples of William Morris' work left for me and so I send three children to the library to bring back all the books on birds, flowers, plants and animals they can muster. Delegation, that's the key. It helps you survive and the kids enjoy the responsibility. Next, I discuss Morris the painter, wallpaper designer, writer and philanthropist and point out the detail in one of his most famous designs, *The Strawberry Thief*. I ask them to look at how the leaves and flowers and thrushes and strawberries all grow out of an invisible vertical line and how the pattern is symmetrical and how the red strawberries on a blue background become a focus and hey! I am an art historian.

I distribute the books and ask them to pick out an animal, a flower and a fruit and to form their pattern around these three. I tell them to make a pencil line down the centre of their page and twenty minutes later, I am reminded of the awesome talents that children have. One boy produces a magnificent work consisting of a scorpion, a bee, and several interspersed palm trees all beautifully symmetrical and interlaced with sweeping fronds. A girl has drawn rich peacocks using its tail feathers and grape vines as an exotic way of filling in the spaces. Everyone is working hard, it's a highly motivated class and it feels wonderful to be able to impart knowledge without the constant need for discipline. One boy is a lazy little toad but the rest of the class are too sensible to let him be an issue. I try to get him involved but he won't have it, so I eventually give up on him like a mother chimpanzee with her dead baby. I can't change the habits of a lifetime in a day, and I wish it wasn't expected of teachers up and down the country.

```
Date: Thursday, 25.01.07
Location: St. Boswells, inside the
 remains of broken dreams
Today's Enemy: Clay ears
```

I walk past a portacabin with a sign on the door that reads 'Inclusion Unit.' The whole cabin should be boxed up and taken as a complete entity to the Tate Modern. It could be called 'British State School Education, circa 2007.' I envisage school parties in three or four hundred years time with wide-eyed kids asking, 'did they really have schools like that, Miss?' It could be used as a prop in a dreadful amateur movie entitled *The Hostile Planet*, or a sensory deprivation tank shipped out from the Vietnam jungles. No sun, alien or otherwise, could ever penetrate the rusty steel plates screwed to the window frames. Over the door hang the sinister words 'Inclusion Zone.' Not quite the 'know thyself' written above the portals of Plato's Academy, but then that was thousands of years ago. Perhaps no one actually enters; perhaps it's just a warning, a bit like the cages full of pirate skeletons that dangled from the walls of seaports. But no, as I round the corner there is already a line of gaunt, blue-white, shaven headed youths metaphorically manacled at the ankle by a chain of mutinous despondency and insubordination.

'Excuse me, sir,' asks one of them. 'Are you in 'inclusion' today?'

'No,' I answer, 'I've been good.'

They go 'hur hur' and slap their thighs and tap their wooden legs and rattle their chains in appreciation.

My indolent chums from Year 10 arrive reeking of tobacco. They bear no malice towards me, though. They posture a bit but that's all. We have come to a flexible understanding, live and let live. Ten o'clock, break time and I snatch a read of the *Daily Mirror*. I used to buy the *Guardian* and the *Independent* but discovered that I never had the time to get past the first page. Besides, the *Mirror* has improved steadily since the demise of the tyrannical Maxwell.

I used to have a cup of tea too but some bastard stole my kettle. Now I just drink water and feel better for it. The next class will arrive in twenty minutes and then it's four periods back-to-back, two and half hours of bronco busting.

By one o'clock, my ribs are aching and I have nothing left to give. I am rung out and steam ironed so I crawl up to the staff room and lay across the five seats of black vinyl to rise just in time for the next double period. There should be twenty-six kids in this class but only fifteen actually make it. I refuse entry to the rest for various acts of idiocy and rudeness. The remainder are hard working kids and are happy in the knowledge that there will be no disruptions from the hounds this afternoon.

3pm and I'm out of there faster than a pig from a pen. It's Thursday and that means Tescos and sculpture. I change into my jeans and feel light and ethereal, it's an unshackling experience. I grab a newspaper and a plate of food and the world is fine. I push my trolley, Margaret's dietary requirements mean that I fill up on mangoes and paw paws and fresh coriander and whole breads and passion fruits and luscious lychees where a soft brown eye appears to watch over me after the second nibble.

I arrive at the sculpture studio around 5.30. It's empty, the course doesn't start until 6. Tranquil. There are works in various stages spread around the room. I roll out a large square of clay and draw the rudimentary shape of an ear on it with a modelling tool. Then I start to build up the ear with the clay. An hour later, it's recognisable as a human ear but the proportions are wrong, the top is too big compared to the bottom and the top rim isn't curling into the inner ear at the right place, also the ridge by the ear hole is in the wrong place and the ear hole itself is an abyss of darkness.

Two hours later I have an ear that is far more satisfying. I see now that an ear is all curves and spirals and mathematical precision, it is an inverted embryo. Only by hands on practice and the passing of time can the ability to produce these curves be assimilated, it is like suddenly seeing the bigger picture, seeing the ear in the mind's eye, a perfect reproduction in three dimensions that can be twisted and turned to any viewing point. This is when the brain and the fingers start working together instead of separately. The class is cosmopolitan; there is an Iranian woman, a Frenchwoman, an Italian, a Spaniard, a German, a Ukrainian, and Andrian who is Albanian. He was taught by the most renown sculptor in the country, a man who can trace his tuition and lineage all the way back to Michelangelo. Hey! Wait a minute, Andrian was taught by someone who can trace his skills back to the great master himself, and as Andrian is teaching me therefore I…whoa there! Let's just try and finish this 'ere ear.

```
Date: Friday, 26.01.07
Location: Elmsfare Wood, somewhere
 over the rainbow
Today's Enemy: Trains
```

My leafy village primary school somewhere over the rainbow from St. Boswells. Here, the kids are pleasant and plump and the parents pump some of that Leeds (the biggest financial centre in the north of England) cash back into their kids' education by providing donations and adventure playgrounds. The day is bleak, cold, wet, windy, dark and it's winter at its worst. I turn left off the motorway and drive down the twisting country lanes to see the strange sight of hawthorn hedges full of cellophane and white wrapping paper, it's all over the road and fields too, then a few hundred yards later I see what looks like a wall made out of flowers. Later, I learn that two teenagers were killed there at the weekend and for a moment I consider how a life can be so cruelly snatched and dashed before it has even kicked in. I also wonder how much second hand carnage, sadness and tragedy you have to witness before you can step out of the shadowy cave and be alive to the beauty in the world. To see, hear, touch and taste it. What does it take to appreciate life at the highest, most sublime level? Is it to live, love and cherish every second of existence in the knowledge that it can be snuffed out like the candle in the wind?

Sometimes, as I exit the motorway and drive onto a country road, I gasp at the sudden appearance of a crimson and mandarin sunrise in a brush stroke sky of amethyst and gold. Sometimes, you just have to.

The class teacher has inadvertently left her diary open. Next to 'planning meeting' are the plaintive words 'Oh God!'

SAS: Supply Ace Special

This is the most challenging class in the school, due mainly to a couple of boys. A few years ago they would have been in special schools in classes of five with a teacher, a supporter, a student, a volunteer parent, a physiotherapist, a psychologist, a dietician, a social worker and a fitness guru. Then the Government fitted several mainstream schools with a couple of ramps and an extra wide toilet and decided that special schools for kids with massive learning difficulties were redundant. Now, I have to teach the exacting Year 5 curriculum to the mainstream kids while Alan and Ryan go waltzing with Matilda.

Alan is a tall blonde boy with a benign face. He has been diagnosed as dyspraxic, a form of autism, but his parents are in denial so he cannot be statemented, which would allow him to receive the extra classroom support he needs. I like him. He has a different angle on life and adores maps and trains. Fortunately for him, and regrettably for his teachers, a distant railway line crosses his vista and lessons are interrupted according to the train timetable with a yell of, 'it's coming! It's coming! I can hear it!' Today though, I am lucky because Arriva are holding a one-day strike.

I try out the successful William Morris lesson and once again it works well, although Alan renounces my schemata of birds, fruits, animals and plants for cheeseburgers, French loaves and chocolate biscuits to create the William Morris Kitchen Collection. Alan has a unique way of seeing things and that's great, I laugh with him but the problem is I have to deal with his exceptional requirements without the support that he would get if his parents faced up to his autism.

Ryan is an even bigger problem. He looks like a wizened old man; fragile and skinny with a pinched face, a dangerously small head and a Gollum-type mentality. Ryan is the embodiment of quantum theory in that he can seemingly disturb six tables simultaneously. I don't intend to be cruel but teaching with these two in the room is like a surgeon trying to perform a heart transplant with two chimps in the operating theatre.

SAS: Supply Ace Special

Controversial maybe, but true nonetheless. Don't get me wrong, I like Alan and even Ryan can be ok in small doses, it's just that the constant drip-drip-drip pressure of having these children in the class quickly burns you out. Their previous teacher left to open a café in Cornwall.

As a supply teacher you are like a goalkeeper in that you are only as good as your last game. You can win every piece of silverware going but if you let in five goals during the next match you could find yourself on the subs bench the following week. One way to ensure that you keep your first team place is to avoid conflict situations, both in and out of the classroom and with both children and adults.

After break, I am due to teach the grid method of multiplying tens and units which is confusing to most. In order to put the method across, I use different coloured marker pens on the white board (much healthier than emphysema-inducing chalk dust.) On the middle table is a caucus of five boys who still get the wrong answer even after the seventh demonstration because they are not tuned in. Meanwhile, Alan questions why the 11:15 Leeds to Huddersfield has not arrived and Ryan is busy re-attaching the legs onto a spider. I should have shrugged my shoulders and given up. Who needs the stress?

I told the class that if anyone got the next one wrong they would do ten at lunch time. Miraculously it worked, everyone got the right answer except for one poor little sod, a real little worker who always gets everything right but this time for some reason he's the only one to get it wrong (apart from Alan and Ryan, who are crawling under the tables and making quacking noises) ands he starts to cry! Not just a little sniffle but great big shaking blubbers and I think - you ogre, you beast, now look what you've done, you've traumatised a small person for life and destroyed any intentions he may have had of becoming an auditor. Fortunately, the bell rings for lunch and when the others leave I try to explain to him through the twin waterfalls of his tears that I know he can do the sums correctly, that it was the boys on the middle table I was cross with and that of course he didn't have to come back and do any more at lunch time and was he alright now? He nodded and headed for the canteen, leaving me nailed to the chair with negativity and self doubt. As a teacher, you must learn to conquer this on a daily basis and instil within yourself a hard core of self-belief, because if you don't you will be sucked into the quagmire of culpability and be torn apart by the talons of doubt while your detractors will seize the opportunity to pour vinegar into your raw wounds of guilt. You must rise above it and tell yourself that it was not your intention or your fault that a boy was upset because he had a sum wrong. You should learn from the experience. So, what did I learn? I learnt never to teach multiplication again and if some of the kids keep getting the wrong answer then: so be it.

The inevitable happened next. Enter the Headmistress, wearing a searching and fretful look having just observed an upset Stu in the canteen. What could possibly have happened, it's not like him at all? I told her that Stu got a sum wrong and to teach him a lesson I placed hot wires on his testicles and beat the soles of his feet with a cricket bat. Not really, but I may as well have.

The 'Good Work Assembly' is on Friday afternoons. It's nice to end the week on a positive high with lots of praise and encouragement for everyone. I am asked to provide the music and so I sing Donavan's *Colours* and *He's Got The Whole World In His Hands*, accompanied by Gordon the green guitar.

3.30pm, it's a wrap. Four different schools in four different areas this week, three primaries and a comprehensive and the dollars are in the bag and I'm out the door.

Date: Weekend
Location: Home
Enemy: Empty energy reservoirs

I usually get back home on Fridays around half four, brew a coffee, pour a brandy and sit down to write. Around half five, Margaret gets home and, it being Friday, I try to push her over the arm of the sofa. She tries to get me over too but I keep my centre of gravity low. At last I lean back over the sofa, faking a slight unbalance, tempting her to take that fatal rush towards me. She falls for it and at the last possible moment I grab her wrists, move to one side and over she goes by way of her own momentum. Sometimes though, she gets me over which is impressive as I'm over six feet tall and weigh two hundred pounds while she is a size ten.

At this time of the week my reservoir of energy is empty to the point of baked mud so we hit the sofa with a couple of DVDs from the school library, first is *Tokyo Story* and then *Bicycle Thieves*. Forty minutes into the beautiful and measured *Tokyo Story*, I fall into an abyss of slumber from which there is no return.

**Date: Monday, 29.01.07
Location: Hinton Valley, the A59
Today's Enemy: the gathering pounds**

A Sunday evening call direct from the Head of Hinton Valley primary. He tells me that Friday's supply teacher lost control of the class and was accused of hitting a child. The incident with Black Teeth and Scraggly Kid was a mere taster of what can happen before things get really serious. Blood drains from my face at the thought of properly being accused of hitting a kid. The mere accusation is the kiss of death because it means instant suspension. We walk on eggshells. In the case of a supply teacher it's a no work no pay situation, meanwhile your hard earned reputation is nuked.

The support worker for dyspraxic Nicholas has slipped a disc and will be off all term. This spells the end of support for the teacher, there will be no replacement, he'll just have to get on with it. You can always tell when a teacher is under a lot of pressure by the state of their classroom. In this case, the innocent opening of a cupboard causes an avalanche of paper and I only survive by breathing through a modelling straw that I poked through the reams that buried me. I've seen teachers crack like this several times; first the paper mounts up and they throw the odd sickie to catch up, only to return to an insurmountable mountain, a veritable Amazon of wasted forest.

The wind howls like a wounded wolf and cuts across the open spaces. The portacabin is creaking and the rusty windows are in danger of blowing in. Part of the avalanche consists of a set of scales that come sliding down the paper piste to land at my feet, leaving me with no choice but to step on them. I look down in dismay at the pointer and refuse to accept they are calibrated properly for they are registering sixteen stone and I think no, that cannot be, because I am only fourteen and a half. I read in the *Daily Mirror* recently about some Australian hackers learning the password of a public weighing machine and adapting the print outs to read, 'you are sixteen stone seven pounds you fat ****!' I feel huge and corpulent and suddenly I'm a fat ****. I slip my shoes off to try to make a difference but sadly, I'm not wearing deep sea diving boots. My self-esteem is plummeting so fast that I go to the toilets to inspect the fleshy blob that is my head. The smell is concentrated ammonia, the light is emitted from a humming forty-watt bulb and the inhospitable mirror elongates my face. I'm not having a good day, and I haven't even started teaching yet.

Literacy is 'The Bees' and numeracy is 'The Alien Invasion.' This is another banker and goes across the curriculum. 'The aliens have landed,' I announce. It's a guaranteed attention grabber, Orson Welles would back me up on this. The lesson involves a large map, pieces of string, jumbled up port names and rulers and it's never let me down.

Lunchtime. The wind is almost lifting the portacabin from its moorings. I sit and listen and contemplate the afternoon. Musical instruments in their respective cases are piled in the corner and provide the inspiration. The first performance is by Bob who bravely attempts *When The Saints Go Marching In* on alto sax. Followed by Ellie on flute; sweet, Vicky on clarinet; brilliant, a spot of keyboard and a dash of guitar, these kids are talented.

Afterwards we watch a video about Victorian factory conditions and how the workers put in sixteen hours a day, falling asleep at their machines and mutilating themselves. I look at the piles of folders, paper, planning files and plastic folders and wonder how much has changed.

The afternoon break is cancelled as the tin sheeting on the roof could let rip any minute. It's becoming unusual for primary schools to have an afternoon break these days. Most go straight through, another throwback to good old Queen Vic.

Kids go nuts in the wind, there are theories that it spooks them or taps into their primal energy. These kids seem fine though, most just play chess and I talk to Nicholas, the dyspraxic kid, about *Lord of the Rings*.

'The *Rings* is visually sensational but is lacking in dialogue. The book is a thousand times better,' he informs me, 'however, Tolkein goes way over the top when he tells you the exact amount of rain drops that fell on the shires on a particular afternoon.'

'What do you think of *Harry Potter*, Nicholas?' I ask, impressed and noting that he has a strong resemblance to Ron Weasley, Harry's main man.

'I do not rate the Potter movie, there is too much missed out. J.K. Rowling wanted too much control of the film, which spoiled it. Films are different to books. She should know that.'

He picked up a knight and a queen from a discarded chessboard and clashed them together.

'How could it have been better?'

'It should have been a musical because a song and a dance routine gives your eyes time to wander over the sets, they were really amazing but passed by too quickly.' He does however rate the novels, 'I've read each one twenty times.'

At the end of the afternoon the Jim Dale look-a-like Headmaster returns and asks if I can come again tomorrow. I accept as it's not often my day gets better after I started teaching.

Date: Tuesday, 30.01.07
Location: Hinton Valley, the A59
Today's Enemy: Gargoyles

7.00am. I unzip a banana and zap on the TV. I don't normally watch morning TV but I want to hear the weather forecast. I take a big bite of the banana and stare at the screen and there, by amazing coincidence, is a chimpanzee also eating a banana and seemingly staring back at me. For some reason I feel embarrassed. Perhaps it's because the 'mirror' is showing that for all my attempts at sophistication I am just a primate at heart.

The ferocious winds of yesterday have taken lives including a woman the same age as me. I'm not being morbid with this life/death thing, it's just that she was killed by a gargoyle falling off a church spire whilst buying a newspaper. This kind of incident always plays tricks with me, I wonder if, somehow, twenty four hours earlier she could have seen the headline 'Woman tourist killed by gargoyle.' Just how innocuous is the act of buying an evening paper? Her death is totally bizarre. It makes me think about life and death again and how a life can be swiftly denied and robbed. It's a fragile existence and the need to keep things in perspective and to never feel trapped is paramount.

On the way to Hinton Valley I listen to a recording of Melvyn Bragg's Thursday evening radio show which is all about the philosophy of happiness. Plato reckons that happiness is the actualisation of a person's true potential. It seems reasonable. I check those scales again, I was right, they are not calibrated properly. I fix it, take off my shoes and my jacket and weigh in at fifteen stone seven pounds, the fastest weight loss programme ever devised. It's still too heavy though, I need to shift a stone before summer so I can wear my swimming trunks under my breasts.

Amy has brought her trumpet to school after missing out on yesterday's musical soiree. During break I sneak a rip on it. I've always fancied a wind instrument. The sound I eventually produce is impressive in its brightness and volume if not its tone. A teacher dips her head through the door ready to unleash her frustrations on some poor kid for making loud elephantine noises.

'Only me,' I say smiling and the seemingly disembodied head bobs back again as if on a spring.

Yesterday the weather was as tempestuous as my stomach after an Indian takeaway but today the sky is pure turquoise and surely it's the first day of spring. Upon arriving at the portacabin, a mysterious redhead thrusts a letter into my hands and darts off again without further ado. I open the missive and read as follows:

> 'Dear Sir;
> Yesterday you refused my Samuel a drink of water from his bottle. It may look like Tizer and it may be in a Tizer bottle but it is in fact water. Samuel said he told you it was water but to no avail.'

At first, I thought it was Samuel's handwriting but decided eventually that it was genuine so I replied:

> Dear mother of Samuel,
> Several years ago, I was once fibbed to by a ten-year-old boy. Ever since then I have remained sceptical of some of the things small boys tell me. As your son is already hyperactive I reckoned he could do without a gut full of e-

numbers. Incidentally, have you ever seen *Alien*? Well, there is a scene in that film where a very nasty thing attaches itself to a crewmember's face; John Hurt's, to be precise. Well I have to say that your son makes that thing seem a bit stand-offish.

Yours sincerely …

At lunchtime, I walk into the village for a pot of tea and a sandwich in a quaint tearoom, the type that would have been popular with the Famous Five. Afterwards, I sit in the village square and enjoy the sunshine. It could be rural France. It's so pleasing that I sing, 'Somewhere over the rainbow, way up high. Birds fly over the rainbow. Why, oh why, can't I?' It's a sweet melody and I am quite into it when I hear a cough behind me. I turn to see an old woman with fluffy white hair, the type you can blow away in tufts to tell the time, grimacing because she can't work out why I am wearing a jacket and tie and nibbling grapes when I should be dressed in rags and clutching a bottle of meths. I refuse to be muted and finish my piece. On the walk back I consider how a woman decides when the time is right to have a tight perm. Probably the same time that a man pulls his trousers up to his tits.

Back at the portacabin the Head appears and to my delight takes half the class swimming. Brilliant. Now I can do an art lesson and keep my blood pressure within safety limits at the same time. First though, it's Kelly on her trumpet. Her first notes gurgle like a Roman central heating system which causes her great aggravation. Ooops! Sorry Kelly, I forgot about the spittle factor.

As they are already learning about the Victorians I apply my newly acquired William Morris activities. They work in beautiful quiet and I have found another classic lesson that is up there with the Bees and the Aliens. The topics on offer in primary schools are universal, whether you live in Bradford or

Billericay. They include the Greeks, Egyptians, Romans, Victorians, Tudors and the Second World War. My brief to teach the latter recently led to problems of a sensitive nature in a local school. Large A3 sheets of paper were spread out on the class teacher's table as she jabbed it with her fleshy forefinger and talked war.

'Today we are doing the Holocaust, but be aware of little Klaus and Daniel,' she said, touching me on the arm, 'Klaus has only been with us three weeks, he's from Germany, you know, and little David is Jewish. Be sensitive. Bye.'

She disappeared then and left me standing in a room that was done out like Churchill's war bunker with gas masks and tin helmets hanging off the walls and models of Spitfires and Fokkers dangling from the ceiling and battleships floating on a sea of blue sugar paper and baco-foil. All that was missing was a large central table covered in sand, toy tanks, and a manoeuvring stick.

I decided to 'be sensitive' by not mentioning the war at all. Instead, we had a music lesson which included *Colours*, *Jailhouse Rock* and *Let's Twist Again*. Klaus and David twisted together beautifully.

Incredibly, three weeks later, same school, same teacher.

'I want you to teach R.E.,' she said, 'we are discussing bereavement, but be sensitive because little Jason's mum has just committed suicide.'

We twisted again like we did last lesson and another child remained trauma free.

Meanwhile, back at Hinton Valley. The secretary asks me if I can come again tomorrow. It looks like the regular class teacher is going down for some time - perhaps he's just learnt that his support assistant has slipped her disc? I can't help them though, I'm booked to go to Leeds.

3.20pm and I'm out of the door. My youngest son is playing football tonight for his school, it's the first game of the season and I want to be there. Thirty minutes later, after giving it ninety all the way down the A59, I arrive just in time for kick off. They win 4-1, it's brilliant. My eldest son is there too. Last year he was the school team captain. They are both good players and if only I can keep them liking me for a few more years I could be in for some nice holidays. Before they go to bed, we play a game where I have to close my eyes and try and guess which one of them it is just by touching their faces. Naturally, I get it right every time, it's a cinch, but they are genuinely amazed. One day they won't be.

Date: Wednesday, 31.01.07
Location: Middletree, by Heathrow
Today's Enemy: Jets

A village school, famous for having an RAF base nearby and the consequent roar of jets overhead. Van Morrison sings 'Gotta get through January, gotta get through February' on the car radio. I empathise with him, February is a bitch but at least it does have Valentine's Day, however if you have no valentine then the bitch is bad. I am greeted by the school secretary, a trim woman in her fifties with bright intelligent brown eyes and an air of controlled mischief. I am reminded of a smart fox. She shows me to the classroom, it's a decent size with views over the open country. The room is full of costumes and props and by the work on the wall I am led to deduce that they are well into rehearsals for Robin Hood.

School productions are nature's equivalent of a heart shaped rainbow. They represent everything good about humanity, a coming together of minds to produce something that is infinitely greater than the sum of its parts. The work that goes into school productions is staggering. The children never forget them; they will forget forty weeks' of numeracy, but not the school drama. My best ever teaching moment happened when I took over from an exhausted Year 6 teacher. It was during the last two weeks of the summer term and the class were described by the Head as 'demob happy.' His brief to me was, 'just keep them under control.'

I decided that the kids had digested enough of conventional work and that it would be a sin to have them leave their primary school full of resentment. I sympathised with them. They are tested at 5, 7, 11, 14, 16, 17 and 18, and they spend all the years in between doing mocks. I needed a theme, something that would bring the essence of primary schools together and which would culminate in a grand finale. I came up with the idea of a circus and began the project with semi-conventional work such as writing about circuses, describing various acts, keeping a circus performer's diary and so on. It began to gather momentum very quickly until eventually the class would hear of doing nothing else. For the next fortnight we made props and painted scenery and rehearsed. Costumes were found, God knows where, for half a dozen lions, a circus strongman, clowns (with full individual make up, the result of another art lesson) jugglers, tightrope walkers, horses and acrobats.

On the day of the performance we built a ring from PE benches and utilised all the gym equipment in the hall. We had music and lights and an audience of parents, teachers and the rest of the school. It was intended to be a one-off, but word spread that a circus was in town and so it was opened up to aunties, grandparents, uncles, nephews and wicked stepsisters and it ran for three nights and when Jenny walked across a beam four feet above the ground and almost slipped the crowd sighed because she was hundreds of feet in the air with no safety net. I don't think any of those kids will forget that fortnight. They will be in their mid-twenties now and I wonder if they ever find themselves smiling for no reason. I do.

I wonder if a similar miracle can begin today. In they come: a Year 4 class. They enter bright as fox cubs, relatives of the school secretary perhaps. An even number of boys and girls, twenty eight all together. I have always considered twenty-six to be the optimum number, providing there are no sads and mads amongst them. When I was their age, I was in a class of forty-four and spent a lot of time with a colouring book. They are well mannered and attentive, a good class on which to try out a new science lesson. Few supply teachers attempt science lessons for lack of apparatus or confidence or both. This lesson will measure reaction speeds and only requires rulers. Their reaction speed is measured by how quick they grasp a released ruler between the pincer of finger and thumb as it drops. For example, if they catch it at the fifteen centimetre mark then that is their reaction speed. Ok, so it's not research for NASA, but they enjoyed it. They draw tables, describe what they did and decide on the criteria that will make the test fair. They are so competitive about getting the fastest reaction that this occurs naturally as in the cry of, 'it's not fair, he's holding his fingers too close together.'

I wonder just how valuable a village school education is. I reckon there is now a three tier system of education in this country, with fee paying schools at one end of the ruler and tough inner-city schools (or 'poor man's schools' as they are known in America, where a great percentage of teaching time is taken up with discipline) at the other, and in the middle sit the little pleasant village schools where the parents are usually affluent and where discipline is not an issue.

At break I am called for duty in the postage stamp playground which is separated from the local cemetery by a dry-stone wall.

'You see that gravestone over there,' says a podgy ten-year-old boy with cheeks you could boil a kettle on, 'the one with the angel with the broken wing?'

I peer across the rows of headstones old and new until I just about work out the one he means.

'Yes.'

'Well, my Granny is in there and she watches over me when I'm at school.'

'Ah. That's nice.'

'Once when I was crying she came over and put her arm around me.'

'Fine…'

After lunch and in between the sound of Phantom jets breaking the sound barrier, I ask the kids about the Robin Hood costumes. They explain about the forthcoming panto and offer to sing all the songs from the show. Magic. Solos, harmonies, counter melodies, extreme wonderment. The day finished with a school assembly and a golden book award and a perimeter of proud beaming village parents all without a hint of hayseed.

**Date: Thursday, 01.02.07
Location: St. Boswells
Today's Enemy: The Taxman**

A learned man once said, 'There are only two certainties in life: death and taxes.' I have to send off my tax form to avoid a fine. I have been lugging a box of receipts around with me for three months now like some penitent dragging a boulder on a chain, but every time I think of those masses of pages and forms and little boxes and numbers I put it off until tomorrow.

The radio cassette in the car is not working for some reason so through boredom I pretend to be an off the wall Scottish stand-up comedian and talk aloud in a laconic highlands accent. The words come spontaneously. I do this for a twenty minute spot and even find myself laughing at some of the content. I tried stand-up comedy once and made a bit of a local impact to the point where I was offered several relatively well paid gigs. Unfortunately, the quality of my performance was inversely proportional to my sobriety and if I had taken that particular path I would have died of cirrhosis very quickly.

St. Boswells again, teaching Declan on a one-to-one basis. I did the same thing a couple of weeks ago when we became advertising executives. This time, he has to write a comparison of two short stories, one from the nineteenth century and one from the twentieth.

'Oh, bollocks!' he cries. 'I effing hate English! How short are these short stories?'

As part of his delaying tactics he shows me a model kitchen he has been designing for his graphics course. It's made from paper cubes, strips of cardboard and a shoebox adapted to form three walls and a floor. He has used sticky paper for the floor tiles and has painted the walls bright yellow. We spend the next ten minutes going over possible improvements in the design of the layout and hey! We are kitchen designers.

But now it's short story time and Declan is not happy. I pick out a story called *Rocking Horse Winner* by D.H. Lawrence, who was also a teacher who retired through ill health. 'Those who can, do. Those who can't - teach.' A famous quote by Lawrence presently being given a government spin. The government campaign to attract more teachers is becoming ever more desperate. They have tried every angle, from the teaching is a vocation slant ('Everyone remembers a good teacher') to the more mercenary but realistic Golden Hello. It won't work. They have even lowered the A-level grades to three F's but still no takers. The only solution is to send press gangs into the wine bars on Sunday evenings. Imagine that, waking up hungover in front of a class on Monday morning and not knowing why you were there. They would fit right in.

I try to make the story interesting for Declan by reading it aloud and using various accents and voice tones but as usual they all end up sounding like a Welsh Pakistani. The story involves a Faustian deal, where the boy is gifted a glimpse of the future whenever he rides his rocking horse. In this instance, the horse who will win the Derby. Declan listens patiently, I can see he's interested because he turns his page at the same time as I turn mine. At the end he says he likes the story and that one scene reminded him of *The Exorcist*. I tell him that his comparison is spot on.

After break we look at the short story from the nineteenth century, *The Imp Bottle* by Robert Louis Stephenson. There is nothing short about this bugger, it seems to go on for eternity. Twenty pages later and Declan is scratching the desk with a Stanley knife. The story is clever but the style is cripplingly boring. The Hawaiian setting doesn't help either, I have to pronounce Christian names like Mauikiuoau and islands like

Koananakukuuluku to a 15-year-old expellee who is becoming increasingly agitated. At last, exhausted by the effort of reading twenty-four pages of close text in several different tongues and trying to keep the lid on the now active Declanukuona volcano, I call a halt with six pages to go.

'That was crap,' announces Declan.

This afternoon we are due at the gym but he's forgotten his kit. I quite fancy a spell of exercise, particularly after setting foot on those cruel scales at Hinton Valley, so I drive him home to get it. His house is one of the few without rusty black metal plates over the windows and rugby could be his way out.

The public sports centre is shared with the school so it's well equipped. First a dozen lengths in the pool and then into the hi-tech gym for five minutes on the tread mill, five on the rowing machine, a few repetitions on the weights and hey! We are professional athletes. We work hard and maybe now he thinks that teachers are not all a bunch of boring old bastards, even though I did subject him to *The Imp Bottle*.

SAS: Supply Ace Special

Date: Friday, 02.02.07
Location: St. Boswells
Today's Enemy: The Scottish Play

After a recent day's teaching I felt battered and bruised and was all set to hit the brandy bottle but hit the clay instead and spent a contemplative couple of hours making ears. I also flicked through a beautiful book called *Anatomy For Artists* and saw why the ear was causing me so much anguish, for it was described as 'a complex form.' I knew it. It was labelled with ten arrow heads naming parts such as the outer and inner helix, the interragic and the lobule. I look at ears now and I see them maybe for the first time. Before I began this sculpture course, they were just lugs of flesh, but now I see the intricacy involved in each and every one of them from the individual lobule to the universal scoop at the top of the ear, the triangular fossa, formed by the Great Sculptor's little finger.

But now it's Friday morning and I'm singing in the car. I lucky dip a cassette from the bottom of a carrier bag and out comes King Elvis who floods the car with a live version of *American Trilogy*. He sings that tomorrow he will die and then all his trials will be over. Then comes the haunting flute part which is resolved only after a piercing scream from a woman in the audience who I guess suddenly realised the poignancy of the words. Next, a huge explosion of percussion and strings and brass before Elvis blasts out *Glory Glory Hallelujah* and a fuse ignites in my big toe and explodes somewhere mid-brain.

The Scottish play has come back to haunt me again. I have been asked to teach *Macbeth* to 9X and if I don't make it interesting, I will suffer a crueller fate than that of King Duncan.

It's time to use all available support mechanisms because as a member of the Special Ace Supply the first rule is survival, or as they sing in the score of *The Italian Job*, 'This is a self-preservation society.'

This class regularly causes me great pain and so I have decided to call in the Welsh Guard in the form of a certain Mr. Hughes, a senior teacher and St. Boswells stalwart. He is built like Snowdon and in the distance I can hear the sound of male-voice choirs and coal hammers and Cardiff Arms Park and Conwy Castle, and the kids hear it too. When he leaves I begin the task of teaching them *Macbeth*.

Fortunately, the start of the play is an attention grabber, the equivalent of a bleeding Tim Roth dying in Harvey Keitel's arms at the beginning of *Reservoir Dogs*.

Big Estelle Richards, 14 going on 45 and as big as a female wrestler on steroids, asks if she can be a witch, 'because the teacher who takes us on Wednesday said I would make a good one.' There are arguments over who gets to be the witches, there are plenty to choose from and heaps of hubble before we even start the bloody thing.

We discuss the witches in terms of how we would direct them in a stage play and answer questions such as; how would they enter? What would they wear? Are they old, young, male, female, a family? What might they be carrying? How will they speak? I feel the lesson is going well. In fact, it's the best lesson I've ever taught. I am proud. I am a teaching machine. I am the frigging lion in the blackboard jungle.

Georgia raises her hand. Georgia is a big lanky red head with gap teeth, a loud mouth and jug ears.

'What is it, Georgia?' I ask, hoping that she is about to confound me by saying something genuine.

'I'm bored.'

Even the least compliant kids blink in disbelief at her gripe. I am wounded but only superficially, for SAS boot camp trained me not to show emotion and to overcome pain in order to continue teaching in true utilitarian style for the maximum benefit of the majority.

At the end of the lesson a few of the kids tell me they enjoyed *Macbeth*. One describes the lesson as 'fat.' One dangerously skinny boy with tattoos and a shaven head comes towards me with a clenched fist but only to ask for a matey knuckle to knuckle jab. Then off they go discussing the merits of William Shakespeare while simultaneously kicking each other up the arse.

Lunchtime. The staff room. A pleasant woman around the 60 mark deflates opposite me. I learn that she has just spent the last hour supervising a Design and Technology class. I listen and respond in the appropriate gaps. She thanks me for talking to her because, 'as a supply teacher, no-one usually speaks to me.' I thank her for talking to me because I am a supply teacher, too. We laugh and exchange stories of the 'what's the worst job you've ever had' variety.

'One of my strangest moments came during a particularly unfriendly primary school's sports day,' she says, 'I was asked to stand on a box in the corner of a three hectare school field and make like a marker post for the afternoon. However, that was balanced out by my experience in a Catholic school. I remember the children working in eerie silence but every now and then they would suddenly raise their hands and ask for a 'sharing moment.' Intrigued, I sanctioned it and watched as a little girl walked to the front of the class and told her chums that she had lost her pencil. The rest of the class then closed their eyes, joined hands and prayed for a considerable time. This was followed by a 'sharing moment' every two minutes which ranged from the desire for a birthday treat at McDonald's to a new set of skateboard wheels. I later found out that the normal frequency rate for 'sharing moments' is about two a term and even then only if the tumour is malignant.'

Moral: kids will take advantage, even if they are the children of the Holy Roman Empire.

An afternoon with Year 7. Not a pleasant end to the week. The first time I took this class, I suspected that I could be dealing with children who were in the throes of demonic possession. It was a nightmare because they had bonded to create a thirty-headed, one-hundred-and-twenty-limbed fiend with one malevolent brain. It was awesome and every time I severed a limb another two grew in its place. It took me three weeks of busting blood pressure to let them see where my line is drawn. Now, apart from the occasional bush fire, they get on with their work.

Today, I even attempted a bit of banter about music and bands. One girl owns up to liking Abba.

'Abba are shite,' opines her friend.

'Listen,' I say, in dull, flat monotones, 'I'm nothing special (pause for effect) in fact I'm a bit of a bore (pause for effect) if I tell a joke you've probably heard it before, but I have a talent, a wonderful thing, 'cause everyone listens when I start to sing. I'm so grateful and proud. All I want is to sing it out loud.' (Pause for effect.) Then, in true Dennis *Singing Detective* Potter style, I fill my lungs with melody and belt out karaoke style…

'So….I….say…Thank you for the music, the songs I'm singing, thanks for all the joy they're bringing…'

They look at me, aghast, but when I repeat the chorus they join in, except for a few who sit stunned and saucer eyed. It's like they've discovered their Grandma performing perfect ollies on their skateboard or their dart playing, football loving, pint swilling Grandpa wearing pink knickers and white stilettos. It's good to keep the buggers guessing.

Date: Weekend
Location: Home
Today's Enemy: Knees

My knee has seized up. A reaction to my workout on Thursday and Margaret's latest tactic of anchoring herself onto my trouser hems whenever I try to heave her over the sofa arm. I have a theory; the only time an individual becomes aware of their physical existence is when they are ill. Could this also be applied to mental health? I'll have to think about that one.

Saturday. We are invited to dinner with friends; a physiotherapist, a psychiatrist, two nurses, an artist and a horticulturalist. If I should choose this evening to have my nervous breakdown, I will be in good hands. The food is wonderful and copious amounts of wine are taken on board and the exchange is as light as the pastry baskets. Occasionally, it veers into the teaching cul-de-sac of death, but I manage to redirect it to horticulture, model making, psychiatry, acupuncture and book binding.

On Sunday we visit an air museum with the boys. The exhibits are set out in twenty four hangars. One is devoted to the bomber crews, with black and white photographs of the crews, most with 'killed in action' written underneath. One showed four gaunt looking young men dressed in flying gear, cigarettes dangling, walking away from a Halifax Bomber after a night on Ops. They could have been walking off a Glastonbury stage. The photo of these ultracool guys brought home the realisation of just how young these heroes were. The average life expectancy of a rear gunner was three weeks.

Date: Monday, 05.02.07
Location: Menton Hill
Today's Enemy: Apathy

7.30am. The agency phones to say that teachers are going down like sparrows over Spain, that they have supply teachers covering supply teachers, and could I work at Menton Hill primary this morning? Fortunately, I haven't succumbed to all the illness that flies about at this time of year, even though I'm constantly subjected to sprays of snot and viruses and bugs and coughs and sneezes, all nicely incubating in a small, centrally heated room. My theory is that by the time I retire, I will either be a complete demolition job or I will have built up an immune system that could allow me to survive in a Sellafield waste dump. Meanwhile, I take a fistful of vitamin tablets everyday and eat lots of fruit and vegetables to mop up those nasty free radicals.

I drive with a heavy Monday morning feeling and my self-esteem is lower than the pointer on the petrol gauge. Sometimes, I feel like I'm working just to keep this car on the road, but that can't be true. (Can it?) When I was working full time, I used to listen to self help tapes when I was driving in an attempt to stop myself disappearing into the quagmire of despondency. I even made my own 'think positive' tapes to play on the way to work – 'Every day you get bigger and better, you are invincible, you are the master of your destiny,' and so on, but in the end I just played *Simply The Best* by Tina Turner. It worked better than anything - anything I ever knew.

I've been to Menton Hill a few times now but I've never been happy there, I'm not sure why. Maybe it's confusion caused by incongruity. The area looks middle-class, yet some of the kids would make a medieval leper appear suave, dapper and debonair. Consequently, I am faced with a mixture of pleasant smiles and squirming Gollums. It is yet another school without a Head or Deputy. Both are off with 'long term illness.'

The first thing I notice is a humming noise similar to the one experienced when standing under a pylon carrying fifty thousand volts. It's coming from a one hundred-watt strip light, which I simply switch off. It's one small backward step for luminosity but a giant leap for my sanity and another example, like the rubberless stools, of the prevailing 'if they don't complain, then don't fix it' mentality. At break, I get nailed for yard duty (surprise) and it's a bollock-shattering zero out there. Unfortunately, yard duty comes with the job in the same way that Ferraris come to pension fund managers.

The first lesson is numeracy. We start by going over the nine times table and I pick up a soft polar bear and throw it at a kid. He looks astounded.

'Whoever catches the bear must answer the question.'

Unorthodox, but it keeps their attention.

I have been interested in theories concerning the different functions of the right and left sides of the brain. Today we expect young children to make the transition between the left hemisphere, numbers, and the right hemisphere, creativity and abstract thinking, in the time it takes to say, 'Martin collect in the maths, Sarah hand out the literacy.' I read recently of some exercises to unify the two hemispheres, something called brain gym, which involves putting the right forefinger on the nose and the left forefinger across the right arm to touch the right ear, then you swap and swap again and keep swapping. I tried it with this class and it was fun, some kids struggled from the beginning and almost lost an eye, but most managed to get into a rhythm. That's when it gets interesting and you see facial expressions of focused concentration very rarely seen in the western classroom. It is also said to have an energising effect, a kind of mental workout. We need more of the esoteric, bring on the Tai Chi.

No planning has been left for literacy so I read a story called *Stone Soup* which involves a stranger who arrives at a village, places three stones in a pot of water and lights a fire under it. The villagers overcome by curiosity appear and ask what he's doing.

'Making stone soup,' he replies, 'but it really needs a few carrots. Does anyone have some?' Naturally, the story involves each villager throwing something enhancing into the pot resulting in the finest soup ever tasted. I get them to make up their own version of 'stone soup' complete with illustrations. They are inspired and work in sepulchre silence, only the inspiring song of a thrush outside the window can be heard. It's so peaceful that at times I drift off into monastic reverie on the meaning of life and decide that the words I saw recently on the side of a battered old white Landrover encapsulate it best: 'One Life – Live It.'

At lunchtime I encounter another member of the Special Ace Supply, Sergeant Dave, who has been on the chalk for years. A few months ago I introduced him to the 'supply teacher as airline pilot' metaphor as in, 'we fly the plane, land it safely and piss off home.' Now, whenever I see him, we talk in aeronautical speak.

'Hi Sarge, how's the flight so far?'

'Pretty smooth, though slight instability during take-off when I had to keep the seat belt warning light on a bit longer than usual. How about you?'

'Fine. Blue skies and a tail wind but there could be a spot of turbulence this afternoon.'

'Oh, why's that?'

'Stag party on board. What about you? Any unruly passengers?'

'One or two, but they have had a warning off the steward.'

'Nothing to warrant an emergency landing?'

'No. It's all quiet now. Lunch is being served followed by an

in-flight movie so I don't expect any more trouble.'
'Good. Safe landings. See you at JFK.'
'Over.'

I'm convinced that Dave stands a couple of inches taller after these conversations, that he suspends disbelief just long enough to get through the rest of a tough day convinced that he is indeed the captain of a Boeing 757, dressed in full uniform and cap and the one ultimately responsible for the safety of seven hundred passengers as he buffets through the ether six miles high.

In the afternoon, it's PE. Statistics say that half the kids in Britain are obese and I note a genuine reluctance for some of the class to get involved. I attempt creative movement while I play the piano; you are a leaf in a breeze, now strong wind, now a hurricane. The response from two exceptionally large girls is the same for each measure of the Beaufort scale. Breeze; they walk slowly around the hall in an anti-clockwise direction, arms folded. Strong wind; they walk slowly around the hall in an anti-clockwise direction. Hurricane; they walk slowly round the hall in an anti-clockwise direction. Arms folded. Meanwhile, some of the other kids are bouncing off the walls and hurtling towards the ceiling via the wall bars.

Incidentally, ask a bunch of kids to run, walk or skip around the hall and they will always go anti-clockwise, at least they do in this hemisphere.

Date: Tuesday, 06.02.07
Location: Elmsfare Wood
Today's Enemy: Arrogant Drivers

I face the road works again. Now I've said this before, but if there is one thing that really grieves me it's the self-centred egotistical bastards who sail down the outside lane until the last possible moment then nonchalantly flick their indicators on and expect to be let into the neck of the bottle because they are superior to the rest of us suckers. What makes me even angrier is the mugs who let them in. In Italy, it would be a shooting incident. In Rome, I once saw an Italian sitting with his hand on the horn while simultaneously reading the newspaper. This morning I turn purple as a Rover suddenly pulls in front of me from nowhere. I give him horn and plenty. More, I edge out of my row of cars and edge and force my way back in front of him again. At this moment I don't care if I lose my entire front end. I stare at the driver and he stares back into the face of a lunatic, then wisely indicates with open palm that I am to resume my fitful and righteous position in life's long and winding road of misery. Victory. Sad, I know, but we are talking principles here, the stuff of wars.

Today, it's Year 5. Alan's class. The blonde dyspraxic child whose mind is through the looking glass. Work has been set but their teacher has left a note saying she doesn't mind 'if I do my own thing.' The work set includes a stifling piece of comprehension dealing with the pyramids. 'Do your own thing' sounds good to me. I try an experiment, a new lesson for me based on *The Jabberwocky* by Lewis Carol. The world of slithey toves is about to be unleashed on a class of innocent village primary school children. After reading the poem a couple of times and writing a few of the words on the board I simply ask the class to have a go at making up their own version and the results are supgarginly sploiv. I particularly enjoyed Alan's attempt:

I asked the Oomigan
To kill the quackadom
So Oomigan set off.
He came to the quavey stream
And the hibby mountains!
He asked Toveni in the haby-haby town
And killed the soliter Oomigan
And the horrible mushti thing died .
'Thankyou Oomigan,' said Daviane.

Date: Wednesday 07.02.07
Location: St. Boswells
Today's Enemy: Road Works & Road Rage

Road rage will kill me. Someone else tried to get in front of me this morning by edging into a gap tighter than my clenched buttocks. He quickly garnered that he was in imminent danger of losing a limb and quickly tucked in behind, so now I have him leering through my rear mirror as we crawl the last eight hundred yards to the land of the dual carriageway (in this case, the 'duel' carriageway) where the real testosterone test begins. At this point, they usually try and overtake but I put my foot down and dip into the red, 'don't mess pal, this is a beamer.' I hold my nerve as the bastard vies to get past me. I'm driving too close to the car in front and the sensible side of me is saying, 'for Christ's sake, slow down and tune into Radio 3.' But I can't hear because of the sound of AC/DC singing *Highway to Hell*. I'm doing ninety but he's still up my arse. He shall not pass. The wind is buffeting the car but it's a big solid bastard, I've got petrol receipts to prove it, and she can take it. I feel the squeeze on my aorta but the squeeze on the accelerator is stronger and he drops back. Jesus, what a way to start the day. Another petty victory on a day when that may be all I have.

Today I am teaching Declan again, he is an hour late but no-one seems bothered. When he eventually arrives we discuss the short stories again because his assignment must be completed this morning if we are to spend the afternoon in the gym. We go over the stories briefly, both have the theme of bargaining with supernatural forces to exchange material gains in this world for eternal damnation in the next.

'Would you buy the magic bottle,' asks Declan, 'to get anything you want?'

I think about it hard and decide probably not. He said he would. I suggest he doesn't consider the prospect of mortality as much as I do because he is young.

'You're not that old,' he says, 'old but not that old.'

Declan is trying to be kind.

We talk about luck and he reckons there is no such thing.

'Do you believe in evil spirits, Sir?'

'There is much evil in the world, mostly caused by greed like we discovered in the short stories.'

We discuss the concept of a soul and the meaning of principles.

'You don't sell your soul and you don't sell your principles,' I said.

'If I sold drugs to little kids to make money, I'd be selling my principles, wouldn't I, Sir?'

'Yes.'

'Well, maybe principles are a version of the soul.'

Hey! We are philosophers.

'Anyway,' I say, 'I'm curious. How come you are in this situation?'

He didn't hesitate.

'There was this teacher, he's gone now, he was a bully - verbally and physically. One day he was dragging my friend, who is really skinny and small, out of the classroom and so I pulled him off. Then the shit hit the fan. I've been away for a year now. Last week the teachers voted against having me back.'

It sounds a rough deal for old Declan but during the telling I have to remove a small screwdriver off him to prevent him carving up the desk. At lunch time I type out his assignment and in the afternoon it is the pursuit of physical excellence. First ten lengths of the pool and then the machines. One is called a stair climber and I grasp the handles which also act as sensors. In seconds my pulse rate is up to 150 beats per minute and red lights are going on all over my system. I slow and stop and it drops to 120bpm but rises again when I merely think of trying it again. I must get checked out. I could be living on a knife edge.

Date: Thursday, 08.02.07
Location: St. Boswells
Today's Enemy: 9XXX

The Year 10 beauties stroll in yawning and stinking of fags. One of them has a gash running the length of his face from forehead to chin, the kind you would expect to find on a medieval knight lying prostate on a battle field, plus a black eye and a bluish yellow nose.

'Jesus. What happened to your face?'
'I was beaten up last night.'
'Who by?'
'I dunno. Can I buy a cigarette off anybody?'
End of story.

My kettle has turned up so at morning break I make a cup of tea in my room and read the paper, or at least try to because a pack of horrible hounds are staring at me through the window like I'm the one in the zoo. I shall ignore them.

'Look at his shirt, my dad has a shirt like that.'
'Look at his hair, it's a right mullet.'
'How old do you think he is?'
'He's drinking tea.'
'Look, he's reading a newspaper.'
'It's the *Sport*.'

That's it. I do not read the *Sport*. I spring for the door and they scream as I sprint down the corridor looking for an exit door. Only the windows separate us. I am reminded of Popeye Doyle driving like crazy underneath the railway line in pursuit of his tormentor in *The French Connection*. I find the exit while they veer left and into the warren of the main building. 'Get out of the way!' I shout to a group of gum chewing girls. The boys run up the stairs giggling insanely and slam the door behind them. I arrive a second later, I look right and left but there's no sign, they know these streets better than me.

Of the two days I teach at St. Boswells, as part of my community service programme, I prefer the Thursday to the Friday because on Thursday I only take 9X for a single lesson whereas on Fridays it's a double lesson and they become more like 9 triple X.

I am teaching them *Macbeth* again because that's what it says on the bottle. The textbooks are in cartoon form and are mightily abridged to leave naught but the sensational scenes and the classier speeches, a bit like the movie version of *Lord of the Rings*. During Act One Scene Five, Lady Macbeth calls on the demons to assist her in her quest of making Macbeth king. 'Unsex me,' she cries, 'come to my woman's breasts and take my milk for gall.'

Giggles and guffaws at the word breasts.

'Sir,' calls out the skinny girl with the sticky out ears, 'My mother is a 42 double D, honest. You'll see them on parents' evening if you don't believe me.'

'Here's a joke,' I say, 'what is the difference between you and your mum?'

'I don't know.'

'You've got big lugs and she's got big jugs.'

I don't say it really but I titter to myself at the notion.

The lesson is interrupted by the arrival of three flashing police cars with sirens on full wail causing a mass rush to the window. I am later informed that a 'mosher' in Year 10 has been running amok in the school, smashing windows and screaming 'KILL THE FUCKING TEACHERS.'

A mosher, I am told, is a kid who is into heavy metal music and devil worship. They say devil worship as if it's only one step removed from collecting football programmes. I'm relieved that he was arrested before he arrived at my class, because due to my Catholic indoctrination I would probably have tried to exorcise him.

Lunch time. I need to download and stretch out across the five black vinyl chairs and escape. Regrettably, I am woken five minutes early due to the clatter of a few dinner ladies who make the witches of *Macbeth* seem like three Hamish women working on a quilt. Only one more class, the villainous Year 8. In they come, cocky as bantams, until I sift out the chaff from the merely chafed and ten of them disappear. Another one arrives late with a promise of sustained effort but in less than a minute he breaks wind, adding methane to the already rich mix of exhaled cheese and onion expirations. I am going to demand that a canary be placed in the classroom. I ship the farter out so that now only his lunch (in gaseous form) remains. I don't know where they go and I don't care because the atmosphere is now life supporting and could grace any fee paying school in the country.

At 5pm, I am in the sculpture studio. I seem to arrive earlier every week. The nights are getting lighter and two cleaners are involved in a lengthy discourse on the durability of mop heads. I can't help tuning in as I prepare to make another ear. It would seem there is more to mopping a floor than I realise, there are flurries, figure of eights, double switchbacks and something called a hip extended side swipe. It is yet another world within a world with its own rules and nomenclature. The caretaker asks me if I would like a cup of tea. I say yes and thank him. A cleaner sweeps under my feet, a young Irish woman. She examines the ear.

'Sure that's marvellous,' she says, 'I could never do that.'

'Two weeks ago I couldn't either. In fact I'm still not sure if I can,' I say.

'Oh you can see it's an ear alright,' she says, hands clasped over the top of her broom shank.

'Thank you.'

'Gessh, it's alright for some,' she says and carries on with her duties until with a final flick of her brush she sweeps herself out of the room.

The lady who teaches my St. Boswells classes on Monday, Tuesday and Wednesday will not be returning after half-term. 'She is going to Spain,' they tell me. I like it. 'Going to Spain.' It's a good euphemism and I will use it whenever I have the opportunity.

SAS: Supply Ace Special

```
Date: Friday, 09.02.07
Location:      Friarton        Primary,
 Wakefield
Today's Enemy: Obesity
```

My intended venue, St. Boswells, are having a Training Day and so the agency have asked me to go to Friarton Primary, Wakefield.

Jesus. Wakefield is an eighty mile round trip plus a ridiculously early start just to find it. Rachael on the phone pleads with me. She's a good kid, and I'm a mug, so it's a good working relationship.

Life in a northern town. As usual, I arrive without maps and rely on a mixture of luck and native cunning to locate the school. It's not easy as many primary schools are tucked into a supermarket car park these days. It's all the space they have left after the local councils have finished selling off the playing fields to the beechwood floor, studio flat brigade. Cat Stevens had vision when he sang, 'Where do the children play?' I pass a school on my left and decide to stop and ask for instructions. Who knows, it may even be Friarton. No, it's St. Aidens. Unlucky. I ring the bell and eventually a woman in a grey smock appears. Late fifties, salt and pepper hair, specs on a string. She is helpful and starts to draw little maps. Then the phone rings and I listen as she tells a parent that her child was an asset to the school and will be missed and that she loved having her at the school and wishes her all the best of God's love for the future. On the other end of the line, somewhere in a northern town, a mother is dewy eyed and smiling.

SAS: Supply Ace Special

With my little map in hand I arrive at a burrow of terraces and there it is, turn left at the Kasmar fish and chip shop just like she said, Friarton. I park and enter the office. A dark haired woman shakes my hand. She is wearing clothes similar to the type the hip-set wore in Leningrad before the eponymous statesman's statue was bulldozed to the ground, that is, black high heeled boots and black stockings with a run in the knee that some men would find sexy.

'I'm not sure which class you are taking today,' she says, 'Year 2 or Year 5. If it's Year 5,' she adds, 'you are in for a cushy day as they are watching a video in the morning and a student is taking them in the afternoon.'

'Wow, it's a giant!'

'Good morning, Year 2. Sit on the carpet while I do the register.'

The first thing I notice about the class is that they all look fantastically smart. They are wearing a uniform which is not the ubiquitous navy-blue but bottle-green. Combinations of pullovers and cardigans complete with school badge and little yellow and green ties. As they sit on the carpet staring up at me with their bright sparkling eyes I am convinced that spring has come early. There is also a support worker in the class for a 'travelling' boy, as well as an Indian lady with a brilliant white smile, Mrs. Singh, who is there specifically to help the Asian children but is generally hands on. The class have been studying the Great Fire of London and are aflame with knowledge. There is a prepared sheet of a street in 1666 and a street today. I look at the date of the great fire of London and see the mark of the beast and…whoa! It's that old Catholic thing again.

I am always astonished by how much six-year-olds know. Maybe they know more when they are six than they will ever know or maybe I'm getting too philosophical. I blame Declan my St. Boswells Ethics Tutor. The morning runs smooth enough. I am nabbed for yard duty but at least they bring me coffee. A tot skips over, looks up at me with his arms akimbo like an illustration from Gulliver's Travels and asks me to race him. For a second, I'm tempted but I control the urge and politely refuse his invitation. Anyway, the playground is too densely populated. I count at least six football games, three skipping ropes, five games of tig, three groups of girl bands working out their latest dance routine, four bear cub scuffles and seven gymnastic displays. Miraculously, there is seldom a collision due to their innate echo location. After break, it's a whole school assembly, a special one as it's the Friday before half term. Gradually the hall fills up with daffodils in full bloom.

'Good morning everyone,' says the Headmaster, 'next week is a special week. Can anyone tell me why?'

He is referring to Ash Wednesday and the start of Lent.

'Yes, Paul.'

'Is it the Queen's birthday?'

'No.'

'Yes, Rosemary.'

'Is it Valentine's Day?'

'No.'

'Luke?'

'Insect week?'

'No.'

'Is it Lent?'

'Yes.'

Big cheer.

Mrs. Singh shares her hymn book with me. I don't know the hymn but it's beautiful and sung in a way that makes the hair on my neck tingle. Mrs Singh sings beautifully and it strikes me as being an uncommon experience, singing Catholic hymns with a Muslim. She was a teacher in India but her qualifications will not allow her to teach in this country. Amazing. At a time when the country is on its knees begging for teachers there is Mrs. Singh working as a support assistant. It's the same policy that does not allow teachers to teach unless they have passed a maths paper, which includes trigonometry and Pythagoras. Useful when you are trying to console a wailing six-year-old with his pants full of shit.

At lunch time I have a sandwich in the staff room. Today there is a buffet and wine because it's the last day of half-term. 'Help yourself,' says the Head, 'have a glass of wine.' I politely refuse because he's not paying me to crash out for the afternoon which would be the inevitable result. A woman with a pair of tight fitting slacks asks me if I play guitar as she saw me carrying one earlier. I nod. She says she used to play bass guitar in a punk band but she hasn't time these days. 'Maybe when I retire,' she adds wistfully, with no trace of irony. Yes, the guitar is a friend and ally, especially with this age group. I told them that the guitar's name is Gordon Green and that he's very nervous after some boys and girls were too loud yesterday. So nervous, in fact, that he will not come out of his box today if he hears too much noise.

The brief for the afternoon is to discuss food with the children and to explain that it is important to eat a healthy diet or risk becoming obese. I have my introductory talk all mapped out in my head, it will involve talking about junk food and in particular burgers and chips that cause fat hearts and breed enormous Americans who can hardly walk. Then I am introduced to the teaching assistant for the afternoon, a twenty stone behemoth with several chins, pendulous gut slapping breasts and hips as wide as the smile of a teacher who has just been granted early retirement through ill health. I rapidly adjust the content of the lesson to the benefits of eating carrots.

Later, Gordon made his promised appearance and they stared at him, awestruck like it was the second coming. I had a wonderful day with these kids and we finished by singing songs. One girl was surely missing a harp because she had the voice of a soloist angel.

'Thank you for teaching us today,' they said with big gummy smiles.

'Thank you for letting me,' I said, and I meant it.

**Date: Half term
Location: Windermere
Enemy: Memories of Marley**

A week off. This is what the job is all about. Any government that tries to clip school holidays will be the one that brings the already dilapidated and neglected Victorian terrace that is State education crashing to the ground. They are not holidays anymore, they are merely breaks between rounds.

On Monday, I head to Windermere with my boys. It's a grey foreboding day but I need to be on the fells under a big sky. Heavy rain has made the main road impassable and we are forced to make crazy detours along winding country roads built for tractors and trailers with buxom rosy-cheeked milkmaids perched on the back sucking straws and smiling coyly.

We arrive at Windermere Youth Hostel and absorb the view from our window, a panorama of the lake and the surrounding fells under a steely sky. It's only 2pm so we have time for a three hour walk. Yesterday, I twisted my back (picking up a sock, such is age) and as a result I am walking with the gait of a rheumatoid chimp but I am refusing to let it spoil this break.

We spend the evening playing Monopoly in the hostel lounge beside a log fire. The boys' financial naivety in the game makes me wince, they are too trusting and nowhere near as ruthless as they need to be to play this game. Perhaps it should be on the National Curriculum in all State schools.

The following day we walk through Troutbeck village, stopping at the local Post Office for a cup of tea. We drink it outside on a bench and look up at the snow on the fell tops. Murray decides they look like the spine of a stegosaurus. We climb a steep track and suddenly we are presented with a view of the lake. Finn points out the sailing boats cutting across it hundreds of feet below, the sun glints off the surface and the world is truly a lovely thing. We head towards it on a bridleway discussing our favourite films, (Casablanca, Austin Powers One and Austin Powers Two, respectively) then circle back round to the hostel. The boys spend the evening playing with new chums, two kids from Accrington and a Chinese boy from Hong Kong, whose parents need a hand cart for their Gucci luggage. I pour a Jameson's whiskey and lie on my bunk with a magazine and read about the mystique and magic of spirals.

In the morning, we manage another walk before heading home fully charged with Lake splendour. On the way back I see a signpost for Marley. Ah, Marley. There is a big shopping centre near Marley where I used to receive lunchtime retail therapy. So how did I come to be teaching in Marley?

Fade out slowly from the present and fade in slowly to some five years in the past.

I am sitting in the staff room at St. Boswells, yes the same one, it's just a richer beige now in memory than in real life. It was my second visit to St. Boswells as I had spent time there 15 years ago. I was teaching maths at the time and my personal world was fragmenting: my wife and I had sold our house and we were temporarily renting one with the intention of buying it. Those plans, however, were scotched when she we got a divorce and she acquired a bungalow and was moving in at Christmas. The chances of getting a mortgage as a supply teacher were grim and so, as well as suffering the break up of my family, I could also be homeless unless I could secure a full time job in the next few weeks. As I had never had a full time job in 15 years of teaching, it didn't look good.

So back in the St. Boswells staff room, I picked up a list of vacancies in the area. There was only one, at a 'Special School' for a Music Co-ordinator. I tossed it back on the table, lit a cigarette (I smoked then) and wondered what I'd do for money after the jury service cover ended the next day. Reluctantly, I picked up the vacancy sheet again and, through desperation, phoned the special school. Mick Jagger answered it, at least it sounded like him, and he told me to drive over and pick up the forms. When I arrived, I was met by Mick Jagger, at least that's who he looked like. We talked about loads of stuff and we laughed a lot and then he asked me if I could do a week's supply work starting the coming Monday.

The classes are small in special schools, maybe seven or eight kids with varying degrees of learning difficulties. The class I was given contained two identical twin boys called William and Benjamin - Bill and Ben! All of them were quantum kids in the sense that, like photons of light, they were everywhere at once and no rules applied to them. I used every trick I had ever learned that week and some more invented on the spot through necessity to keep them from tying me up in Gordian knots. At one point, I had them 'dressed up' and sitting in a make-believe bus while I desperately thought of songs to sing whenever the 'bus' 'stopped' at another place of scenic beauty and wonder. Mick liked it, he liked it a lot and he asked me to work the following week as the teacher of this class had phoned in sick. No wonder. It was Friday afternoon, Monday seemed a lifetime away and besides, I needed the money so I said OK.

Monday morning came and the prospect of driving the magic bus for another week seemed to be a surreal option. I did it though and I went back again the following week and halfway through it I was interviewed for the job of Music Co-ordinator with four other baton wielders. I was awarded the post and was now a full time teacher for the first time in my life and I was earning money during the holidays with two extra points for teaching in a 'Special' school. Hey, Mr. Mortgage Man, give me that mortgage because hey! I am a Music Co-ordinator!

The summer was mayfly ephemeral and in what seemed a flutter of a fragile wing it was time to take up my new post. The first day of the new term was a training day and, so in early

September in bright sunshine, I arrived at my new school feeling quite career minded. I had come to terms with the fact that I wasn't going to be a rock star in this life but that, with application, I still had time to make a heroic contribution to education.

I was met in the car-park by a deeply furrowed Mick Jagger who said that there was a lot of serious shit flying around and he would explain more later. At this stage, he didn't give anything more away and so I sat in the staff room, bemused, as did the others who had received the same information. Eventually, Mick told us that the Deputy Head would not be coming this morning as he had been given a 15 year prison sentence for child abuse.

Gasps and screams of horror and disbelief. One woman passed out and slithered from her chair onto the sticky carpet while a grown man wept. Meanwhile, I am looking for hidden cameras in the belief that I am the victim of some sick cable TV show.

The situation was to get worse. Three weeks later Mick Jagger was also suspended for similar unrelated charges. His live in partner, it later transpired, saw an opportunity to drop him in the shit from a great height and told police he had interfered with her young daughter. Mick was completely exonerated, but it cost him his job. He didn't mind though, he was given early retirement with ten years' enhancement while the rest of the staff were given a life sentence in a different prison.

Mick was replaced with a tyrant and a bully of the highest order and well known to union reps as the bastard's bastard. His physical appearance alone was intimidating, being several stones overweight with a boozer's complexion. He was a product of the machine, a growing infestation that was ready to die for the party, a link in the Ministerial chain of fear where everyone was responsible to someone and no-one was responsible for everyone. He and his kin were sent out to bite ass and any poor wildebeest who couldn't swim across the great swirling river of bureaucracy was chewed up and shat out by the saurian bastards who lurked in the murky waters in ever greater numbers. The fat bastard (as he became known) tried to implement six years' worth of paperwork in six weeks. This involved four meetings a week that always began with a catch phrase question that went, 'How do you eat an elephant?'

Answer: 'one bite at a time.'

Ideally, he would have liked the staff to chant the answer to his question. It was bollocks anyway as he was forcing the staff to eat a whole hind quarter and tusk at one sitting.

By this time, a lot of the staff were on Prozac. Those that weren't were drinking heavily and people who had stopped smoking years ago started again and spent their breaks and lunchtimes in a makeshift smokorium in the boiler room. Then to really put the pressure on, the Authority came and said they were going to close the school down. The mental health of the staff began a downward spiral then but the tyranny continued and everyday they were under the cosh. The whole situation was bizarre. I was in charge of the harvest festival concert with a brief from Pol Pot that it had to be the biggest and best festival ever because the parents needed to see that everything was under control with him in charge. This led to some interesting spending. On one occasion, he organised a 'musicologist' to spend a day with me writing songs. She flew up from London and stayed overnight at the Hilton - and all to spend 45 minutes tapping out a melody on the piano that sounded like an inverted *Chopsticks*.

The harvest festival was a success thanks to the kids and the staff who worked like galley slaves on boat race day. The fat bastard looked kindly on me after that triumph but it was short lived. The next day he announced that the Ofsted inspectors were arriving in two weeks for an 'extraordinary' inspection and that all planning and individual education plans would have to be on his table within the week.

'Take a look around,' I said, 'these people need a break.' He glared at me over round wire spectacles and his hatred was palpable. He said nothing, just simmered, but I knew he would bide his time. It came a couple of weeks later with a Mafioso-type speech that went something like this: 'The Authority want to see you tomorrow. Unfinished business.'

That was all. He turned and left. I remember loading my car up that night with boxes of files when I suddenly thought, No! I returned to the school, barged into his office and told the fat bastard what I thought of him and didn't wait for a response. The 'unfinished business' would remain unfinished because it was six months later when I returned after being off on the stress ticket.

Elephants have long memories though, and as FB was the size of an elephant, I knew he wouldn't forget. Indeed, on the morning of my return he told me that an advisor from the Authority was arriving the following day to observe my teaching. The advisor was a real slimy, toady smarmball prick who held his clipboard like a shield. At the end of the first lesson, he was unable to pick any gaping holes in my method but insisted that my letter G's were not rounded enough!

He slithered out then and headed to Fat Bastard's office. There was a room next door to the office that was always empty and so I put my ear to the wall. Their exchange was revealing and sinister because they were discussing my professional assassination. At the time there was an agreement between the Authority and the Unions for a policy of 'no redundancy.'

'When this school closes down he will have no job but will still be drawing a salary,' hissed the advisor.

A nice thought, but completely untrue. The bastards were being vindictive and malicious on a personal level.

'We can't have that,' said FB, 'we'll nail him for incompetence. I'll issue the formal papers tomorrow.'

I'd heard enough. I told the secretary that I was having a mild heart attack and needed to seek attention immediately. It wasn't far from the truth. I took another three months off sick but, on the advice of my union rep, I returned on the very last day of the summer term, which was also the last day of that particular school's existence, in order to answer the incompetence rap.

We met in FB's office, the five of us: FB, the grease pole advisor, the NASUWT rep, a female personnel officer and me. The union man began the proceedings.

'You are the white rabbit,' he said looking at the insipid advisor, 'you are the Queen of Hearts,' he said to the tweedy personnel, 'and you,' he said, looking directly at FB, 'must be the Mad Hatter!'

FB turned purple and tried to bluster a sentence but nothing came out apart from a few flecks of spit. He had been made to look preposterous and the outcome was that I would be found another school at the end of the summer holidays. It was brilliant. The Authority would have their revenge though, the following two years were spent on a tempestuous voyage of madness around some of the stormiest schools in Leeds, ending where this bit of the story began in Marley.

Fade back in to the present. When I arrive home, there is a message from my ex-wife to say that an old friend is in town with his family and they would like to meet up for a drink. I hadn't seen him since I was his best man twenty years ago and I walked to the arranged venue remembering the times we had together. It's good to see him, he's bald but that's to be expected and it's strange talking to him after twenty years and feeling that it was only a few days ago since we'd been rolling around the floor arse holed at yet another party. The easy humour and the piss-taking just carried on from where we left off and time is meaningless. The only evidence of it passing being his lack of hair, my corkscrew stance and the four living, breathing, free thinking beings opposite us. He teaches in a private girls' school in Shrewsbury and tells me that the only bit of challenging behaviour he has to deal with is when one of the girls accidentally lets a door close behind her. He asks me what it's like working in the State sector. I go to the bar and buy some drinks.

```
Date: Monday, 19.02.07
Location: Briston
Today's    Enemy:    Javelins    and
   Juveniles
```

A few weeks ago, I met a brother Special and we exchanged horror stories. He told me he had recently been sent to Briston Comprehensive school to teach PE but went AWOL at lunch time. 'It was like trying to get wild lions to jump through fiery hoops,' he remarked. So this morning I receive a call from the agency offering the teaching of PE at the same place. Unable (and unwilling) to interfere and influence the fickle finger of fate, I have no option but to say yes. At least the school is local but it's in a part of town where bus drivers fear to go. I arrive at the school in time to attend the morning briefing. This one is like something from NYPD.

'Kowaldsky, you and Mulligan patrol the chemistry block. Moroni, you and O'Hare take a look at the workshops. I heard there could be something going down. Stanislavsky and Denisovitch, check out the foreign languages sector.'

'Hey c'mon man, that place is bad.'

'You don't like it, Denisovitch, you fothermucker, then hand in your Cert. Ed. and take a damn hike.'

I am wearing a newly acquired tracksuit and hey! I am a PE teacher. I approach a young woman who is wearing shorts. I can't help noticing that her legs are very brown and long. My hunch is that she is either a member of the PE department or a very popular history teacher. She tells me to head towards the sports pavilion at nine o'clock. Ok, but first I have a class to register. I push my way through a gauntlet of fists and knees to the classroom door. It's locked and I have no key and the kids are getting restless. A big bruiser of an Aussie teacher, transported to England for stealing a pig, pokes his head out of his classroom door and tries to calm them by calling them 'uglies.' It's no help in opening the door.

I go in search of a caretaker and return ten minutes later but the class have flown and I am left flapping with an unmarked register. Bells ring and classrooms disgorge their contents and I am suddenly an old piece of driftwood bobbing along on the rapids of youth. Eventually, I am dumped outside the gym and slightly dazed look up to see the woman in the white shorts with the long, tanned, shapely legs walking slowly towards me just like the girl in *Dr. No*.

'It could be a bit disjointed today,' she says, 'because the two male PE teachers are on a climbing-wall course.'

She smiles sheepishly, picks up a sack of hockey sticks and sways towards the palm fringed beach.

Meanwhile, outside the mesh glass doors stand three long rows of testosterone producing machines. I estimate their number to be anything between seventy-five and one hundred and because two teachers have 'gone up the wall' it's up to me to teach all of them. What can I do? Play fifty-a-side, in a re-enactment of the Mongolian cup final where the teams are on horseback and the ball is a goat's carcass? The prophetic words of doom from my brother-in-arms Special float like spectres above my head. He probably had a similar experience and I begin to suspect that the two male PE teachers are not on a climbing course at all but are, at this very moment, digging a tunnel underneath a vaulting horse.

In these situations a member of the Special Ace Supply cannot afford to display any weakness. Respect will always be given to the male with the strongest smelling piss. Once that has been established there will be order and discipline. I must not show fear, not a whiff of it. I stand tall and immediately put down the hint of an insurrection sharply and unmercifully by refusing to let the instigators take any further part in the lesson. Three sullen youths, who had the temerity to wheeze, are not happy with the decision but I cannot relent on my judgement because that would be construed as weakness; fatal in a situation where I have to control three different games of soccer on three different pitches.

Incredibly, I manage to control the situation until the last five minutes when a violent contretemps between two opposing players results in a flurry of blood, tears and flying snot. The perpetrators are noted and reported and somehow it's lunch time.

In the afternoon, I am to teach javelin-throwing techniques to a mixed group of Year 11 kids. I have studied the technique over a cheese sandwich and now I lead a thirty strong band of primitively armed teenagers. I am tempted to raise my spear in the air and shout 'Mazambula!' but the sight of those deadly weapons focuses me and the javelins are released one at a time while the rest stand way back.

'Can we throw them when and how we want to, Sir? We usually do.'

'Not today, son,' I answer as potential shish kebab.

3.30pm. The last javelin is thrown, it rises, drops and slithers harmlessly across the grass. I have survived and am in need of a long glass of something cool, yellow and fizzy.

Date: Tuesday, 20.02.07
Location: St. George's Comp.
Today's Enemy: Physical exercise

This sporting life. It's fortunate that I invested in a tracksuit because I'm teaching PE again. Today I'm at St. George's Comp, another local school. I sometimes wonder what happens to the thousands of kids I have taught. I should be a local celebrity by now. 'Hi, sir! Remember me? I used to fart all the time, you nearly gagged once. I'm an accountant now. What are you having?'

It's been ten years since my last visit to St. George's but I knew I'd return one day for I am Comet Man and St. George's is in my orbit. By coincidence, the last time I was there I taught PE for a five week stint. Nothing has changed apart from Jim, the PE Supremo. Man, he's changed. Ten years ago he was olive skinned, black moustached and whippet thin after playing three full games of football every day. Today I hardly recognise him, it's embarrassing, he looks knackered and he's only fifty, grey as a badger, a moustache like the residue of an ice cream and a green and purple shell suit with a cigarette burn. He should have been rested years ago, but now that they've closed the retirement gates he'll be demonstrating the correct way to perform a triple vault on a zimmer frame. The first lesson is Year 10 football and we are both involved which is a bonus as I'm still recovering from yesterday's Tajistani Cup Final.

We stand outside the door of his private changing room, the one with the shower tray full of basketballs and spare kit with spider's webs around the taps. It has a certain odour, a toxic mix of athlete's foot powder, stale sweat, scuffed leather, plastic, liniment and an imprecise nuance of a certain something that makes the difference between a regular smell and a great smell. It's a cologne that saturates the senses at a subliminal level and which will later cause life hardened adults to inexplicably stiffen in horror at the slightest suggestion of any sport that involves participation.

Now comes the passing over of crumbled notes, ostensibly from parents, which Jim ritualistically crushes and tosses onto a yellowing mound. The potential skivers are duly directed to an appointee who dishes out various sizes of mud caked shorts and hardened T-shirts. Only one boy remains.

'Goodier,' says Jim. 'You are a human medical dictionary. The boy who put the con in hypochondria. Goodier, the Anti-sport.'

Goodier hands over the neat envelope and Jim reads the contents to the sniggering group of 15-year-olds - 'Dear Sir; please excuse Graham from PE this week because he has bad diarrhoea - bad diarrhoea,' repeated Jim, 'what you want is the good sort son. Fair enough, you stay here and keep warm. Would you like some chocolate?'

Goodier nods enthusiastically.

'Ok, spell diarrhoea and you can find a nice cosy place in the mat cupboard to eat it but if you can't…'

Goodier joins the kit queue.

'Why do you bother, Goodier?' Jim calls after him, 'You never get away with it. If you came here with a missing leg I'd still make you do the hop, skip and jump.'

The boys laugh, even the ones sitting blue-white and shivering in a T-shirt three sizes too small for them.

'I can't understand it,' said Jim, 'you lot don't want to do any mental activity and you don't want to do anything physical either, it's like trying to teach bloody trees.'

'I wouldn't say that, sir,' calls back a dark haired lad, 'there are some physical things we like.' The others laugh.

'I don't mean that kind of physical activity, McClements,' says Jim, 'anyway, you ought to try it with a girl sometime.'

The boys laugh again.

'Ok,' says Jim clapping his hands, 'it's cup final day.'

'You're not playing are you, Mr. O'Connell?' Asks a nervous Goodier. 'I'm still limping from last week.'

'That was a fair tackle Graham,' responds Jim, 'I would have given myself a red card if it wasn't. I'll just ref this week, promise. Neutrality is the word.'

It's bloody freezing and the cold hacks like an ice-pick but at least I'm wearing track suit bottoms and a fleece, unlike the poor little sods who now have goose pimples the size of golf balls appearing in prehistoric protest on death white legs. Jim is wearing a sheep-skin coat and balaclava.

'This way lads,' comes a muffled shout, 'think warm.'

The ground is as hard as the socks on Jim's radiator and coated in a late frost.

'Line up quickly,' shouts Jim over chattering teeth, 'I've lost boys in these conditions, seen their toes drop off and worse, keep moving. You pick first, Foxy.'

At the end of the team selections, two little knock kneed kids are staring at their boots and trying to stave off hypothermia by wrapping their painfully thin arms around their ribs.

'You can have both of them,' shouts Foxy to the other team captain and the pair, with their self-esteem in irretrievable tatters, shuffle off to take root in some other part of the field.

'Foxy's team play in red, so swap shirts,' calls Jim, over his scarf.

The boys reveal their torsos to the bitter north wind and shudder as they toss over the stiff shirts.

'Let's get fluffin' started,' shouts Jim, 'before my toes turn black.'

For a few minutes Jim watched as Foxy's team went one up, then two, then three and then the warrior spirit in him could stand it no more.

'I'm playing for Anderson's lot,' he yells.

Foxy screws up his face.

'You play for us, sir.'

If Foxy thinks this will even things up, he is sadly mistaken. Game on.

'Foul,' screams Jim as Anderson is sent flying. 'Free kick, I'm taking it, get up Anderson.'

Jim lofted a perfect cross onto a lethal shaven head.

'3-1,' shouted Jim.

Now he was animated and although the balaclava stayed on the sheepskin came off but only to reveal another half dozen fleeces. The ball landed by chance then at the feet of one of the little knock kneed kids and Jim was on him like a terrier.

'Foul,' screamed Foxy but Jim was the ref and the ref disagreed.

Jim passed the ball to Anderson who struck it hard on the volley and it screamed into the top left corner. Beautiful.

'3-2,' called Jim punching the air while Foxy limped back to the centre.

I like to think that I displayed a bit of latent class but my bursts could not be sustained, the ice cold air cut into my lungs like cheese wire. Jim was warming up nicely though, the one time triallist for Sheffield Wednesday still had it and as the game continued his fleeces were shed like snake skins until eventually he was down to his T-shirt, a level that he had obviously not been expecting to be at until late Spring as the print of a huge pair of tits under the headline 'I love my Sun' proved.

'What are you all staring at?' Shouted Jim, 'This is the new Liverpool away kit.'

Jim was twenty-three again and the cup was up for the taking. Three minutes to go and one goal behind.

'Pass,' shrieked Jim. Anderson crossed the ball and Jim, as if refuting Newton's laws of gravity and the natural laws of the aging process, climbed to meet it.

Bang. Jim's bull neck lunged forward and the little keeper never stood a chance. In celebration, Jim stuck out his arms and weaved down the pitch in Spitfire mode.

'It's not fair,' protested Foxy, 'he always fucking does this.'

Jim turned on him, said nothing just stared manically and Foxy became one of the few to catch a glimpse of life after death should he even think of raining on Jim's parade.

Jim was going for glory, this was the day when he would gain the respect of the kids big time and have an easier ride for a few more months to come. He might even achieve the accolade of, 'Mr. O'Connell, he's not a bad old twat,' and no-one was going to spoil it.

Foxy retrieved the ball from the net and took it to the half-way line again, sensing by now that this was no ordinary game and that old O'Connell wanted desperately to win this one. The look on Foxy's face indicated that he was going to make sure that he didn't win it even if the big bastard crippled him. Jim willed his body into action, knowing that tomorrow he would be unable to get his socks on without assistance, but tomorrow was tomorrow and today was today.

Foxy's face contorted into the mask of youth claiming their place and time. 'Come on,' he rallied, slapping a few narrow backs, 'let's fucking do it.' Jim ignored the language; he was focused on something greater. Foxy gave a short pass and received it back. Foxy was good, wasted on this team, he was bloody good, he chipped the ball over Anderson and ran on past him.

Jim knew his defence was pisspoor, consisting of the two knock kneed kids who would have been much happier reading comics and drinking Ovaltine by a warm fire. Foxy would waltz round them. Anderson might have stopped him but Anderson was still on the ground. Foxy had five yards on Jim, if he scored again then it would be all over because the only thing that Jim had in his lungs now was pride.

Jim's heart dissented but he raced after Foxy with steam coming out of his hairy ears. Foxy took it round one, then two before running into what felt like a brick wall and Foxy's nose burst like a ripe tomato all over Jim.

'Sorry son,' said Jim, offering a helping hand which Foxy refused. 'Free kick to you.'

Foxy spat out a stream of burgundy phlegm before unleashing a shot that smacked off the post into the bemused keeper's gloves.

'Craig!' screamed Jim, racing up the line. The keeper punted it and Jim chested it down, Anderson half nodded with approval and shouted for the ball, he was in a good position, Jim fed him and ran on while Anderson gave him a quick one two and Jim was in possession again with only one defender and the keeper to beat. Anderson moved to the far post and called for the return ball but Jim was not for passing and moved forward deftly with the ball between his feet. 'Slide him!' screeched Foxy and a muscular 15-year-old lunged forward but Jim, dropping his shoulder with surprising grace, sent the youth the wrong way.

Jim was at the end of the penalty area, he pulled his hefty thigh back and unleashed a mighty miracle towards the goal, the crowd held their breath and then roared as the ball thumped into the net. Jim fell to his knees and sucked in air and dribbled sticky spit like a stricken bull. He was locked and frozen in position, cast in bronze and I saw the pathos of it all. Here, set four square on the green fields of England, was a man who had fought and won his last battle against mortality.

Jim stared up at the circle of boys through streaming eyes and tried to speak through snot and bubbles but the words wouldn't come. The boys began to laugh and the laughter soared until it became one continuous ear splitting note and they walked off the field leaving him where he fell.

A few flimsy snow flakes floated down and one landed on his damp grey moustache and from the touchline the boys observed the helpless frozen monument to a sporting life in sudden silence and waited as their emotions fought for supremacy. I asked if he was ok and he nodded and raised his hand as if to say give me five minutes.

The boys on the touchline began walking back towards us led

by Foxy with his nose like a crusted jam tart. The rest followed and soon the whole group were gathered round in silence.

'Give us yer hand, Sir,' said Foxy.

Jim looked up and smiled and I felt sure that at that moment a light entered his heart that would sustain him for years to come. Together, we managed to carry all eighteen stone of him back to the changing rooms like primitives bearing a tribe sustaining catch.

After school I went to check him out. He was reading *The Sun* in his perfumed boudoir.

'Look at the knockers on her,' he said.

'Nice,' I said, 'see you around, Jim.'

'Hey,' he said, 'did you see that goal?'

Date: Wednesday, 21.02.07
Location: St. Boswells
Today's Enemy: Outdated education systems

My bag is packed with swimming gear and tracksuit all ready for an afternoon in the gym with bad boy Declan. I am psychologically prepared for an easy civilised day, the kind that hundreds experience every day. It's a lovely feeling and I sing *If I Was A Rich Man* all the way to Leeds. Upon arrival, I am informed that Declan will not be in school today and I am to cover for a Geography teacher who has gone home ill.

Bastards. What a sickener. The sky is elephant grey and the temperature is achingly cold. I loathe this place even more than usual. The first lesson involves fifteen minutes of bronco busting while the class get used to the idea that I am not their regular teacher. Eventually they settle down and I have the chance to observe them. A Year 11 class whose body language is that of those who have entered a room with a sign above the door that reads 'Abandon hope all ye who enter here.' One of them is wearing headphones and is in a trance; his hair is long and dirty to the point where lumps of congealed grease hang from it. I had long hair once, but mine was washed regularly and could even be luxurious at times.

The work set for this group is to plan a campaign for the creation of an environmental area around a newly built reservoir. They have as much interest in the project as a vegan has for a tongue sandwich. A few minutes later, the door is opened and it's show time. Two girls appear, both chewing gum with a vengeance. One is short, blonde and plump and the other tall, skinny and dark.

'Sorry we're late, sir,' says the blonde and she sits down and crosses her dumpy legs and shoves her hands into her leather coat pockets. The skinny one sits sideways and disappears behind the curtains of her long straight hair. I'm sure there used to be an old music hall double act that involved a couple of gals just like these two where the short one spoke for both of them and whenever she spoke to the tall one it was in the style of a patronising adult talking to a blind man.

'Don't mind us, sir,' says the blonde, 'we're as thick as two planks us, we haven't been to school for months, have we?'

She glances at the skinny one who is no more than the tip of a nose peeping out of the hair. The idea of asking these two to contrive salient points for the creation of an ecological development programme is ludicrous. I realise that we are wasting these kids' time and it's wicked to impress our shit on them. The argument for vocational studies in schools has never been more obvious. I ask the girls if they enjoy geography and the answer is plain, simple, direct and honest.

'No, sir. It's crap and boring, isn't it, Linz?' she says to her beaky friend. The curtains twitch in agreement.

'So what would you rather do?'

'I want to be a beauty therapist.'

She gives a big smile and I think, yes perfect, she would make a good one; pleasant face, big personality, so why isn't she learning the rudiments of it now instead of wasting her time, and everyone else's, writing about a non-existent reservoir? Do we delude ourselves that we're giving them more options in a future life, or are we actually giving them more options in a future life? Genuinely? At some point, we may have to be brutally honest, and ignore our middle-class guilt.

I then ask her friend what she would prefer to do instead of geography and as expected the blonde answers for her.

'Nowt, she doesn't want to do nowt.'

Problem: what do you teach a kid who doesn't want to do nowt? Perhaps the truth lies somewhere in the double negative. I ask another girl at the back what she would like to be when she leaves school.

'A hooker,' she replies. 'It's £100 a night and all you have to do is wank, spank, suck and fuck.'

It was the impassive way she said it. She could have been talking about a routine office job. We take dictation, keep the place tidy, send letters and select files. Type, wipe, lick and pick. I'm not shocked anymore. She's not saying it for effect and she's not trying to front me out. Whatever, I am suddenly paddling in murky waters. I tell her primly that I would rather she didn't speak like that in my presence.

'What's the matter, sir?' She asks. 'Don't you like it when I talk dirty?'

'Just don't use that language in my class.'

'But it's true,' she protests. The lads are sniggering now, all except the greasy one who remains oblivious due to the micro earphones concealed behind his chip pan hair. Later, I consider that she meant it. Working as a prostitute was a serious career option for her.

At break time, I visit the staff room and drink a contemplative coffee when a lardy bloke with a crumb infested ginger beard sits down beside me.

'Are you still teaching English on Thursdays and Fridays?' He asks.

I nod.

'It's tough here,' he says.

I smile.

'"What does not destroy me makes me stronger," Friedrich Nietzsche,' he adds and then departs.

I think about the quote. There is sense in it but only up to a point because sometimes I feel that because of my seeming exterior resilience I am in danger of being destroyed by my own strength. It may be safer in the long term to be weaker because to be weaker and to suffer a complete nervous breakdown could save me from the effects of protracted stress. There is no such thing as a 'sudden' heart attack.

Date: Thursday, 22.02.07
Location: St. Boswells
Today's Enemy: Knife Attacks

The Year 10 lads and I have an agreement. If I don't make demands on them, they will not make demands on me. Today is *Stone Soup*, and one boy's soup consists of a bottle of rum, two ounces of 'special' herbs, one eighth of resin, two pills, flour, milk, a fistful of magic mushrooms, a nip of snow and a stalk from Jamaica.

At break I scare the shit out of myself by reading *The Daily Mirror*'s investigation into crime in Britain, a catalogue of horror on the streets of Britain from the sleepiest rural village to the nucleus of the inner city. By the time I have finished the piece I am ready to acquire a 'Are you feeling lucky punk?' Magnum 45, a shoulder harness and a spring mechanism for my wrist. 'Are you looking at me? Are you looking at me? Well there sure in hell ain't no one else around here…'

The river of crime flows throughout Britain. I remember one class, a Year 9, when I was teaching advertising techniques. The class had straggled in. Straggled, a word that has become as inextricably linked to the way schoolkids enter a classroom as the word slippery is to eel.

However, the way to a kid's heart is often through their sweet tooth and so the opening question 'What is the world's most popular sweet?' focused their minds enough to advance to the next question of 'Why is it the world's most popular sweet?' (It's a Kitkat, if you didn't know.) The answers flowed like a hot chocolate river and included:

The sweet is bought by all ages;

Because it is in fingers it can be shared;
Its name is easy to say, short and sharp;
It is in red packaging which attracts the eye;
It is beautifully wrapped in foil;
It is like buying yourself a nice present;
You don't have to eat it all at once;
Good adverts;
You can keep the rest in the foil;
It isn't too expensive;
It is a nice mix of chocolate and biscuit;
And…as said by a particularly scrawnbag of a kid, without any tone of facetiousness or attention seeking behaviour: "You can use the foil to freebase crack cocaine."

Not any more you can't, smart ass. They no longer use foil much to the chagrin of Rio Tinto Zinc who have no doubt seen a fall in share prices since the decision was made.

But the truth of *The Daily Mirror*'s river of crime was to get much worse.

A recent stabbing revolved around the possession of a bull terrier, seemingly a status symbol amongst this age group. This led to several youths repeated slashing and stabbing the victim while at the same time being urged to do so by several ululating girls chanting 'kill him, kill him' while dressed in school uniform. Another involved a youth being chased off a bus by two thugs and then stabbed to death. It seems that knives are the weapon of the moment and like some tribal totem they gain in potency if they taste the blood of a life at its most vital. Knives are becoming fashion accessories and that prospect is terrifying for they are not difficult to acquire. The average kitchen contains enough cold steel to satisfy any vicious blood lust. Dip your hand into any tool box and you will extract a potential weapon. Come to think of it, as my SAS training has taught me, a soup spoon can be a lethal weapon in the wrong hands.

The courts need to be quick to react to this tide of knife attacks. Educating is valued and valid but it takes time, meanwhile some serious heavy duty sentencing is necessary to deter young people away from life under the knife before we see any more corteges of funeral cars and tear stained text messages.

With a *Daily Mirror* induced shudder, I recall a couple of years ago at a school in North Yorkshire giving a bollocking to some youth who was barging through the dinner queue like a demented scrum half. He stared at me with poison in his eyes before eventually slithering off. I was lucky, that same afternoon he carved someone with a knife and was expelled.

I put *The Mirror* down and try to put it from my mind. The next class arrive, Year 8. 'I'll kick your fucking head in,' exclaims a scruffy little sod to an even scruffier little sod and so I immediately ship him out. One down, but echoes of *The Mirror* come back to haunt me.

At lunchtime I lie on the floor at the back of the classroom and sleep for twenty minutes. I learnt this survival technique when I was posted to a special school for teenagers with behaviour problems. The call came on the second day of the Autumn term. I was still recovering from my time as the Music Co-ordinator at the asylum where, after three weeks of that environment, I couldn't even co-ordinate a pair of socks. What made this new posting particularly interesting was the fact that the school was undergoing repairs and therefore half of the boys were to be taught at a country mansion!

I arrived at the commandeered stately home after a two hour drive and a drive up a long gravel track to a large Victorian mansion complete with wonderful mosaic tiled floors, sweeping staircases, long curving banisters and baronial sized wood panelled class rooms. I was introduced to a few members of staff and everything seemed to be quite pleasant.

Then the taxis started to arrive. The boys that were disgorged from them were devils with dirty faces, everyone of them sucking hard on a cigarette. This is the end of the line. Soon the air was ringing to the sound of expletives used only to shock.

I think at this point I may have thrown an internal safety switch to prevent any further damage to my cerebral cortex because from September until Christmas that year I more or less played the part of a UN Observer. The tension was incredible. It was like trying to keep particularly nasty bull terriers apart. The boys would kick off at the slightest provocation. I remember a bizarre English lesson supporting a woman teacher who was trying to teach six 14-year-old boys the finer points of Romeo and Juliet and her answering questions such as, 'Did he fuck her, miss?' with a, 'No, I don't think he did fuck her. At least not on the first night.'

I remember driving another woman teacher home after her wrist had been snapped like a brittle twig by a six-foot nutter. I remember the squeals and shrieks of a boy as he writhed in agony and spurted blood over the beautiful blue of the mosaic floor after being smashed in the teeth by another boy. I remember delicately putting my jacket over Dominic by the road side after he had jumped off a ten foot wall in order to escape his pursuers into the path of an oncoming car. I remember seeing his leg bones appear through the macerated flesh of his shin and riding with him in the ambulance to the hospital. I remember how the same kid had pinned me up against the wall and tried to bite my nose off and I remember my car that night with every window smashed. I remember the staff locking the doors and phoning the police as the kids battered at the door screaming murderous threats. I remember taking them on a Christmas trip to Disneyland Paris where reality finally succumbed to fantasy and I remember finding a secret room in the old country house and locking the door and lying down beside a radiator to try and escape the madness every lunchtime through sleep. I also remember whimsically jetting off to Barbados at half-term for a glimpse of a paradise that will surely be mine in the next life.

Back at St. Boswells, which is a considerable distance from Barbados, one of the classes I normally teach are having a visit from the police, a PR thing where the police try to show that they are not the enemy. Instead, I am down to cover a Year 11 class in the computer suite. I have a flash of trepidation as it could be another 'Houston, we have a problem' situation, but as it turns out the class is the top group and are sorted, sensible and mature. Also, there is another member of the Service in the class. I recognise him by the tattoo on his left arm that reads 'Who Dares Teaches.' Two Specials in one class adds up to an administrative error, but neither of us is inclined to report the matter. His name is Daniel and he is being seconded from the Kenyan Government to study for a PhD in Education. Daniel does a few days supply teaching to boost the grant. He is immaculately dressed in a mustard coloured jacket, light blue shirt, orange tie and green waistcoat, and he is very soft spoken and refined. I ask him how he finds working in Leeds as opposed to Kenya.

'The children in Kenya would never be rude to a teacher or come into the classroom making a noise. In Kenya, there is the utmost respect for teachers and they still administer corporal punishment,' he answers.

There are those who think the cane should not have been abolished in this country either, but personally, I didn't become a teacher to get involved with sadomasochistic practices. If caning does return then it may have to be carried out by an outside agency with the employees heavily vetted. It could be called The De Sade Corrective Punishment Agency.

'There are similarities though,' continues Daniel, 'recruitment and pay, for example. Teachers in Kenya eke out an existence. When I return to Kenya, I will be given a good job in administration and I could perhaps get you a job, too.'

Mmm?

Thursday evening is my sculpture class, a parallel universe and an elixir to a week's teaching. I start by making another ear. It still doesn't come naturally though. I do some more work on the model of my son's head but I have a problem getting the eyes symmetrical. By the time I finish it, my son will have a big, white beard.

```
Date: Friday, 23.02.07
Location: St. Boswells
Today's    Enemy:    Wind    (of    the
  external variety)
```

The wind is gusting at a reported 80mph and I literally have to push against it. It's like a supernatural force trying to turn me away to greater things, but what can possibly be greater than teaching in yet another heart of darkness? The wind has created a twister of crisp packets which threatens to envelope me and carry me over the portacabins to a land somewhere over the rainbow where the roads are constructed from bright yellow brick. It is quite a spectacle of sight and sound because coke tins are also revolving at a furious rate. I would stay and watch but it's too dangerous, I could be struck down by a flailing child.

Year 10. Damien surprises me by working as he usually does sod all. Today though, for some inexplicable reason, he has produced two pages of writing on starting a band. Earlier, I visited the library and took out every book on pop music on the shelves, the idea being that the boys could use them for writing inspiration. Damien's writing is all to cock and the spelling is of a Year 2 level but he has made an effort and that's a big something. He tells me that he's written hundreds of stories, usually in bed for a couple of hours before he goes to sleep. In your dreams, Damien.

I take 9X into the library to watch a video of the first act of *Macbeth*. It's a brilliant attention grabbing opening with a battle scene straight from *Gladiator*. The language still tests them though and they struggle to focus. Julia eventually gives up on it and produces a lipstick and does her lips in a rude shade of pink to win the attention seeking contest against a passionate Lady Macbeth.

After lunch, it's the Unteachables, Year 7. I must 'screw my courage to the sticking place.' This class is a seething pot of unstreamed liabilities containing at least ten kids who are special needs. I send five of them out immediately. The remainder of the lesson remains calm and I achieve my aim of going home on Friday with my blood pressure intact for the weekend.

Date: Weekend
Location: Cosy town pub
Enemy: Small Talk

The chances of me attending a Special Ace Supply 'do' would normally be the same as me picking the winner of a horse race, i.e. one million to one, but not only am I SAS through and through, I am also a war correspondent and it is my duty to report to you all aspects of warfare - so, for my sins, I go. Upon arrival, I receive a sticker from a woman who reminds me of a young Julie Walters. Up until now she has only been a husky voice on an early morning phone line. The Specials are clustered together and look cowed. Almost immediately, I give up any attempt to join them and head to the bar for a magnificent pint of real ale.

Fortunately the beer is superb and I get drunk and play the piano and generally make an arse of myself, although I do come to the rescue of one old dear who looks around the eighty five mark. She is tiny and too small to reach her coat. I offer to lift her up so that she can reach it, but she suggests that it may be easier if I just hand it down to her. It turns out that she is still teaching and making a good fist of it! I mingle and meet up with another pensioner, one of the hang 'em and flog 'em brigade and I think, Jesus, get a life. If you retire then stay retired. By 9pm only my pilot friend and a woman are left. She tells me that her son, now nineteen, still has a poem called 'Yellow' on his bedroom wall.

'He wrote it for you when you came to teach at his primary school,' she tells me. Ah! Suddenly, the night is saved.

Date: Monday, 26.02.02
Location: Hiatus
Today's Enemy: The Ice Maiden

No work booked today which is extremely unusual. I use the time to reflect on some of the stranger experiences I have had during my time as a member of the elite. This includes a posting to a school for children with profound disabilities. In retrospect, I don't know how I lasted the term. I was practising Tai Chi at the time, maybe that helped.

My class consisted of six children with either Downs Syndrome, autism or some other condition. Edward was autistic, a ship trapped in a bottle, an able pupil with a brilliant attitude and academically streets ahead of his peers, but socially inept to the point where making eye contact was an impossibility. Samuel was also autistic and displayed traits of obsession and echolalia (the repetition of words.) He had a brilliant memory though and always won the memory games we played. Lorraine was a pretty girl with dark hair and large brown eyes and big red ribbons but mentally she was extremely limited. Jessica was dressed by her mum to resemble a little old woman and was intellectually poor and Terry was relatively bright but again suffered from some syndrome that was academically debilitating.

Sarah's story was particularly sad. She was the only survivor of a car crash that occurred when she was a baby. Now, at the age of eleven, she was capable only of saying 'Ba!' This was a sound she used with varying degrees of intensity to signify pleasure or displeasure and all emotions in between. She had a lovely face and would often go into a great fit of infectious laughter. At lunchtime, I used to push her to the canteen and spoon-feed her.

The screams and wails in the canteen could be disturbing. One boy was always freaking me out. You can't call it a tantrum because of his situation but that's more or less what it was. He would suddenly go berserk and flail his stick like arms and kick his plate into the air while the other children put their hands over their ears. Then he would scratch and grab at anyone in front of him. Usually, it was his teacher Sandra who on one occasion was heard to scream, 'help! He's got my nipple!' Sometimes I would try to prise his fingers from her hair (and her nipple) but his strength was awesome. Then he would pogo and lash out with his fists. There was always a danger of infection as the poor kid used to play with his own excrement and the residue would be lodged under his fingernails.

The saddest place of all was the class where the children were incapable of even sitting up. Some of these kids were deaf, dumb and blind and could only feel touch, or at least it was assumed they could feel touch. They were like big-eyed baby birds, helpless in a nest and dependent on a helper for everything. I was responsible for music in the school and often these children would be pushed in to 'listen' while I played the piano. Here, they were placed on special frames that allowed them to remain periodically vertical, essential to ensure proper circulation. The frames were placed around the piano while their helpers took a break for twenty minutes or so leaving me in charge. The situation was both tragic and surreal and yet within the confines of this caring environment perfectly normal and nothing that an evening with a hip flask couldn't overcome.

Incredibly, there was more bureaucracy in this school than any I've ever visited, due in the main to The Ice Maiden who drove several of the staff to despair through her constant haranguing and bullying techniques.

I have seen a teacher covered in bleeding scratches from a recent confrontation with an epileptic child being bollocked for not having her French planning done properly. French!

She and I rapidly developed the kind of relationship that made the one between McMurphy and Nurse Ratchet in *One Flew Over The Cuckoo's Nest* look idyllic. At the end of term, I had given all I could. The work was harrowing and incredibly difficult on all levels and once again I remove my fedora to everyone employed in these places. Not only do they have to contend with the daily emotional battering of working with such heart-rending and challenging children they also have to overcome the handmaidens of the Government in all of its admin-crazy, interfering madness.

A few weeks later, I was asked to teach in another Special school. It was a similar set up but this time with older children. I was reluctant but as it was only for a week I said yes. On my first morning, a boy with Downs Syndrome (who was built like a giant cannon ball) shot across the floor and rugby-tackled me at the knees. I have walked with a slight limp ever since. I decided after that to stop working in Special schools, as to teach in those you have to be a very special person indeed.

Date: Tuesday, 27.02.07
Location: Elmsfare Wood
Today's Enemy: February

I enjoyed my day off despite the foul weather. Back to reality now though, or at least to Elmsfare Wood and a Year 2 class. A lorry is in danger of tipping over in the gale force winds just in front of me. Ah, the demons of February. This is the second time I've had this class. There were tears last time from a little girl who reckoned me for an ogre but this time she's calm and composed. There is no support on offer so it's just me and 27 six-year-olds.

Fortunately, they seem well trained and I might just survive the day without turning purple. I write a few simple words on the board and get them to put them in alphabetical order; if they finish, they get to draw what the word is. Easy! A few stories and a double act with Gordon the green guitar and I'm heading for home in the hammering rain. Life kept simple. Just get up in the morning, go to work, come home, have dinner, watch TV, go to bed, keep your head below the parapet and you'll be ok. Just watch out for the gargoyle.

**Date: Wednesday, 28.02.07
Location: St. Boswells
Today's Enemy: Power Plays and Parental Problems**

Another day with young Declan. I have been thinking hard about these sessions for I am on the horns of a dilemma. It seems that most of the staff do not want him in the school. To the unions, the case is black and white, he hit a teacher and therefore he must go. Declan's version is that the teacher was hurting his friend and that he merely went to his aid. I have discussed Declan's situation with a few teachers, most think he's an arrogant little bastard. The RE teacher reckons he should have another chance, 'we all fuck up sometimes,' he says, quoting from the good book. The real problem as far as Declan is concerned is the power struggle taking place between the Unions and his grandfather. Meanwhile, my brief is to get him to complete an essay discussing how the modern film director helps in the understanding of the text of Romeo and Juliet. We read the first act together, taking alternative parts.

Big rugby playing Declan gives it his best bard with his baseball cap screwed round to the side of his head and periodically we stop and decipher what is actually being said. I try to put myself in the boy's situation: if I was fourteen, what would I make of 'an hour before the worship sun peer'd forth the golden window of the east?' I would have been overwhelmed by the language. However, if I had been taught by an adult who didn't appear to be from an entirely different planet and who took the time to explain it, then perhaps the crocodile-infested river of class divide could have been bridged. Maybe Declan's grandfather would like the present situation to continue for some time, for at the moment Declan's one to one education is the costliest in the country. Even at Eton the fees are not £30k a year.

Next we watch the film version of Romeo and Juliet directed by Baz Luhrmann. It's an impressive movie and Declan was hooked in from the start. Shakespeare would have been a good Bond director, he knew how to grab the audience by the balls with a quick blast of tension and violence. The spade work with the text is paying off as the language now has meaning and Declan is telling me that Benvolio has seen Romeo an hour before sunrise. The sun peers forth from the window of the east as I fast forward in time and see Professor Declan chairing a meeting of educational reformers and flying the flag for all the council house kids who never had the benefit of a one to one education.

After lunch we go to the gym for a couple of hours. I start on the running machine for five minutes and am forced to confront my mirror image and the extra pounds that are strapping themselves to my gut as the years slap by. The diet never worked, I am still twenty pounds overweight. I spend half an hour each on the bicycle and the cross-country skiing machine, which is a killer, fortunately there are built in heart sensors on the grips which tell me that my pulse is already up to 140 and red lights are flashing in heaven. I back off and raise a few weights and become mesmerised by two perfect female buttocks clad in tight black lycra moving up and down on a steps machine in a perfect rolling rhythm. I feel fine after the work out but I always aim to underachieve as I once almost killed myself on a treadmill by trying to beat the machine.

Late afternoon and I go to watch my youngest son playing football. It's the return leg with the team they played last week. It was tough last time with my son's goal deciding the outcome. It was even tougher this week, but with a couple of minutes to go, he does a repeat of last week and they snatch victory. Yes!

In the evening, Margaret and I visit the theatre to see Steinbeck's *Of Mice and Men*. The production is brilliant and afterwards, over frothing pints of Guinness, we discuss it to death and carry on discussing it at home with a bottle of wine way past midnight just like real adults do.

'Tell me about the rabbits…'

Date: Thursday, 01.03.07
Location: St. Boswells
Today's Enemy: Familiarity

I am becoming a regular at this place. Too regular. I am gaining a strange respect purely out of familiarity. Some of the kids shout at me as I walk by and these days it's not always abuse. Big Estelle calls out that she likes my cowboy boots and I just smile. I have had these boots for twenty years now and I keep getting them soled and heeled. I only wear them on occasional days now though, like today when they reached out for me as I dipped into the shoe basket and I thought 'Yeah, why not? I am an individual, I am not a number, I still have spirit, don't dig my grave with a JCB just yet!'

In fact, several of the kids pass comment, 'Cool boots, sir!'

'Thank you. They belonged to my dad Clint Eastwood.'

'Oh yeah. I like that song.'

My Year 10 chums arrive wearing their usual deodorant, a reeking mix of tobacco and body odour. Anthony is chewing on a cheese sandwich, I ask him to eat it outside and to make sure he eats it all as the boy is skinnier than an anorexic whippet.

I came across a thought provoking article recently about why it's important to give children the opportunity to write creatively. The writer referred to two boys who had recently seen their team win the FA cup. The boys wanted desperately to express how they felt about it.

Eventually, after clenching and unclenching their fists several times, they spurted out that it was, 'just fucking brilliant.' The writer went on to say that words are needed in order to escape the confines of the self.

Having said that, I think 'just fucking brilliant' would be a just fucking brilliant way to feel.

So this morning I strive for a lick of creative writing from the chums based on the story of the three wishes. I read the story and they get to modify it but it doesn't capture their interest. Scott appears industrious but when I look he has just copied out the words from the example story verbatim like he always does. I have a plan though and it involves a thesaurus and a competition: 'Describe how you felt when you had your first nicotine hit.' It worked a treat.

After break, 9X. I show a video, the Roman Polanski version of *Macbeth*, which is much gorier and consequently better received. Perhaps the same tactic could be used for all the classic English novels - introduce sex, blood and violence in gladiatorial dollops in order to grab and keep the attention. *Jane Eyre* could definitely be enlivened by a good splurge of gratuitous Technicolor brutality, and the image of Elizabeth Bennett riding a white stallion into war is precious, too.

I get to sculpture class early again, almost straight from work. The caretaker makes me a cup of tea. I get the clay head of my son out of the 'wet room' and start on the ears. The past few weeks of making single ears has paid off. The hitherto fleshy lugs stuck onto the side of the head now have form. I know all about the triangular fossa and the tragus and intertragus points and they no longer scare me. Soon, I have fashioned two fine-looking ears and now I want to work on the mouth and soon discover that the mouth and lips are as difficult as the ears and I must spend the next few weeks making mouths before I return to the head.

```
Date: Friday, 02.03.07
Location: Elmsfare Wood
Today's Enemy: Paranoia
```

The traffic jerks along in a series of epileptic fits. We drive in a bubble world where noses are picked and genitals scratched. The prolonged road works have given me the opportunity to learn all the words to the song *If I Was A Rich Man* from *The Fiddler On The Roof*. I sing it loud and give free reign to gestures. I especially like the bit that goes, 'Lord who made the lion and the lamb, you decreed I should be what I am, would it spoil some vast eternal plan if I was a wealthy man?' This morning I unconsciously take my hands off the steering wheel in order to embrace the beseeching plea in its entirety.

A Year 1 class. Hey! I'm the children's entertainer, 'Uncle Mac.' All I'm missing is a big red nose and a spinning bow tie, or maybe just the bow tie. I was actually juggling three apples today while simultaneously looking at my watch to see how long I had left, like some old stager on an 'end of the pier show' doing the warm-up for Mr. Marvo the all-conjuring, fire-eating, sword-swallowing, mind-reading escapologist.

Teaching a Year 1 class is like walking on wren's eggs.

'Mario is on double rittolin today,' they tell me, 'and the twins are diabetic. If they go into a coma…'

Once again I take my hat off, in this case a top hat with a flapping lid, to the teachers who teach Year 1 full time. At least with Year 4 and above I can ask them to write a story and then re-attach my retinas for ten minutes. Here I have to resort to advanced story telling techniques and rely heavily on Gordon the green guitar. If I request a spot of quiet, I am ignored but if I tell them Gordon is getting a migraine you can hear a pin drop into a bucket of feathers. The diabetic twins are scarily identical, two girls with swishing side pigtails. They are very confident and good fun, being just the right side of mischievous.

I read them *Stone Soup* and get them to act it out. There are theories that children learn best when they are active. Personally, I find it easier to keep them moving because when they are sitting at their tables it does my back in bending down to help them. After break, we head to the hall for Scottish country dancing which I make up as I go along. This is followed by an art lesson that is totally unconnected to Scottish dancing but linked, rather cunningly, to *Stone Soup*. It involves drawing pictures of various foods then writing underneath what they are. They work diligently, but only for ten minutes before they start to lose it again, because that's how it is with the dolphins of the human world.

During lunch break I close my eyes and download for fifteen minutes. Later the teacher in the class next door asks why I never go to the staff room. I tell her it's nothing personal and don't mention that it's because it's only the size of a basketball player's shoe box and I always feel like Gulliver stepping over feet and canteen trays of cheese pie and sloppy custard. Also, it seems like the staff expect a bit of entertainment from me; Uncle Mac, a saucy adult version.

I told them a few weeks ago about my idea of starting an 'Elvis Presley Ghost tour' and that has kept them amused ever since. I think it could work actually, not that I'll ever find out. Like most teachers, for the past ten years I have come up with all kinds of weird schemes that will 'get me out.' Last year I had a vampire cloak made for a proposed Dracula Ghost Walk; it is presently mothballed and in waiting. Other schemes have involved a 'Big Kind Auntie' agency where retired women come to your house and bake apple pies and sew buttons on your trousers. My best scheme so far though is to stand on the street corner with a sign that reads 'Make me a millionaire!' I reward all contributions by letting them fill in another square with a red felt tip pen. I imagine the scene where I am up to the £700,000 mark as I relieve yet another American tourist of a fiver while he praises me for being enterprising in the way that won the West.

The evening weather is wicked in the original sense of the word, grey, freezing and pissing down and I'm watching my oldest son play a gutsy game of football as he takes the ball round two players and slots it in the goal. He tells me that he's been chosen for the lead part in the school play and that he's received a credit for French. Brilliant. I told him recently to show them what he can do but I'm not so naïve anymore, tomorrow he could receive a hundred lines.

'No homework has been set tonight,' he said with a grin.

'Don't worry,' I said, 'I'll set you some.'

Grudgingly, he set to while my youngest son battled with his piano scales.

One day they will thank me.

Date: Weekend
Location: Borders Bookshop, York
Enemy: Gervais Phinn

Margaret and I dined on vegetable korma taken with a pleasant bottle of red and then watched *Brief Encounter*, courtesy of the school library. The film is a brilliant piece of work, showing how a speck of dust can lead to an innocent's steady descent into hell. The cinematography plays its part beautifully by highlighting Celia Johnson's face to make her look either quite manically fiendish or perfectly vulnerable and serenely beautiful. The trains hurtling through the station add to the tension and provide a metaphor for its star-cross'd lovers: their trains are always travelling in the opposite direction. Then there is the music, the perfect accompaniment, Rachmaninov's second piano concerto, and it's all filmed at Carnforth station.

A few years ago, I took Margaret to Carnforth station as part of a romantic weekend. The station was completely dilapidated and run down. The subways are still there where Trevor Howard emerged from the bowels of hell to claim his latest victim.

On Saturday I go to a book signing session given by one Gervais Phinn. I am interested in this man because he is making a fortune out of telling stories about visits to schools in a certain part of Northern England. He's a talented man, but his sanitised stories are a slice of unreality which seems to be popular with those who want to be deceived. However, in true unpublished tradition, I thrust a couple of chapters of my work into his face and run. A few days later he writes to me with the following advice, 'Find an agent.' Thanks for that, Mr. Phinn.

Date: Monday, 05.03.02
Location: Blairtop
Today's Enemy: *Spartacus* imitation

A village school. The Headmistress phoned me at home yesterday afternoon and then spent ten minutes telling me how to teach perimeters to a class of Year 6 kids - she is obviously mentally ill. Eventually, I started thumping the table and told her there was someone at the door.

For a change, it's a pleasant drive involving no major road works. I head towards the moors and some very good walking country and arrive at the school for 8.30am. Clusters of daffodils are ready to turn the school banks yellow. I am met by a peacock of a woman who I bet was a real groovy chick in the 60s. She has that kind of Isle of Wight festival feel about her, but unfortunately she has been addled by a lifetime of teaching and that Jimi Hendrix guitar solo is her last clear memory.

Today I will witness chaos theory in practice. I am determined to stay calm, however, for if I lose it and the adrenalin pumps in then I am ruined. The first lesson is swimming and so it's back ten miles the way I came, only this time I have my fingers in my ears as I try to catch up on Act 2 of *Macbeth*. The noise levels are potentially damaging, it is akin to trying to read on an airplane runway.

I am given the top group, they are accomplished swimmers so it's a matter of giving them a good workout and some fine tuning on the strokes. The water is inviting, the ripples on the pool are Hockneyesque or maybe Monet-ish. I remember a couple of years ago, I was asked to show some paintings of Monet to a Year 2 class. I showed them one called *Le Grenouilerre* ('*The*

Frog-pond.') 'Just look at the water, how real it looks,' I said.

'It looks like you could put your finger in and it would come out wet,' said a particularly observant seven-year-old. I looked again and thought, shit he's right, and then I thought, wait a minute, how is Monet achieving that? I saw then that he had managed the effect by slashes and strokes of paint.

Afterwards, we did the same thing using pastilles and the results were so inspirational that for the next twelve months I read everything I could find about Impressionism and in doing so discovered a world of brilliant artists which included Mary Cassat and Berthe Morrisot. I even took up the palette myself and completed thirty pictures. They were passable, but perhaps more important than the finished result was how I felt when I was doing them regardless of the outcome. I felt good, all peaceful and relaxed. Reason enough to one day return to the watercolours.

The kids leave the pool to make space for the next school, Felton Street primary. I worked there a few years ago. The staff were very close having spent something like three centuries at the place between them. It was as if the Addams family had managed to get a school together. There was Harold, the elderly science co-ordinator who made the Nutty Professor seem like an anally retentive sub-librarian. His forte was the making of rockets from fairy liquid bottles. Launch day was always a big occasion, almost as grand as a Royal marriage. Five, four, three, two, one, whee, whoooosh!

All eyes looking skywards, hands shading eyes from the glare of the Houston sun.

'About how high up will it be now, sir?'

Only I noticed Harold scooping the still very grounded fairy liquid bottle, now split like a banana skin, into an already prepared carrier bag.

Then there was Barry, who looked more like a village blacksmith than a primary school teacher. He wore a white shirt, a clean one every day, no tie, open collar and rolled up sleeves to present an unfeasibly large pair of hairy forearms. The blacksmith said little and was extremely wary of strangers. Eventually though, after I had been visiting the school sporadically for ten years, he whispered that he had something to show me. Twitching with curiosity, I was led to an outbuilding whereupon he unlocked several padlocks and, as each one fell open, my anticipation increased exponentially. Inside, laid out in front of me, was the biggest train set in the known universe and Barry stood like a proud father and let me drink it all in.

'Twenty years,' he said, 'twenty years it's taken me to put this together.'

I said nothing, just continued to absorb.

'This is the second one,' he said, 'the first one was wrecked by vandals seven years ago, almost to the day.'

He stared ahead and clenched his fists and the muscles on his big arms rippled like shoals of piranhas at the memory. I got the feeling that if he had caught the perpetrators in the act they would now be part of the paper-mâché embankment.

'Come up here, you'll see better,' he said.

I followed him up four wooden steps to a control desk complete with a galaxy of flashing lights.

'There's about six miles of wire under that layout,' said Barry, rolling up his shirt sleeves higher, 'I work on it most nights, last week I finished that power station. See those cooling towers? There's no steam coming out of them, yet.'

I laughed, thinking he was displaying a sense of humour.

'There will be though,' he said grinding his teeth, 'I've been talking to Harold about it, he reckons we can use dry ice.'

'Good idea,' I said, checking the exit.

Then, like the great architect himself, he began flicking switches and the whole show came alive. It was a scaled down version of RailTrack, the main difference being that these locomotives were all moving on schedule. Trains zipped through town, country and city, through tunnels and past disgruntled and disillusioned commuters. Detail laid upon detail, even down to conductors in day-glo orange waistcoats holding banners demanding parity with the drivers.

'Now watch this,' said Barry pointing at the track with one hand and giving his nose a quick squeeze with the other, 'see the two 125's, one going south and the other heading towards Edinburgh via York.'

I nodded. The trains were hurtling towards each other and a head on collision seemed unavoidable. I could almost hear the screech of brakes and the sound of searing metal, I could smell the sickening stench of cascading fuel when, at the very last moment, he flicked the points and the trains rippled past each other on the diagonal like two coral snakes. If Barry had just fired a bullet through the middle of a silver dollar with a Colt .45 and was at that very moment blowing the smoke from the barrel he could not have looked more smug. Unfortunately, he ruined the mood almost immediately by saying, 'You won't tell anyone about this, will you?'

I promised him I wouldn't.

Then there was Maureen, the Grand Dame of Felton Street primary school. She had a big Auntie relationship with the kids, most of whom came from backgrounds that were as rough as Desperate Dan's chin at 5pm. Often you would see the kids in her class handing round a huge tin of toffees while she told them about the war from a first hand perspective; she was a land army baby. Maureen was also famous for her musical input. She was even the subject of an article in a broadsheet newspaper dealing with her campaign for traditional singing lessons. She was actually a brilliant pianist who could play the most demanding stuff, rehearse an entire Year 6 production and simultaneously discuss the benefits of Meltus for chest congestion without dropping a demi-semi quaver.

The Panto was the highlight of the school year for Maureen. The rest of it, including the irksome SATS (stress, anxiety, trauma) tests, were just something to be somehow got through until the next one. Maureen's class tended to be one trick ponies that no-one else could teach. Boys as big as small trees and as hard as blue brick would purr at her feet and dreamily unwrap sweets as she told them about the day her mother pricked a crashed Luftwaffe pilot up the arse with a pitchfork. Supply teachers in her class were like Christians tossed to a pride of ravenous lions.

Then there was Ed, the master of cynicism. I remember one assembly when the kids were singing like angels, 'Think of a world without any flowers, think of a world without any trees la la la…'

'Excuse me, Maureen,' interrupted Ed, walking to the front of the hall to address the school.

'Right! Now think of a car without any paint on it because two boys in this school have been reported to have been climbing over them.'

Silence.

'Well, has anyone anything to say?'

Silence.

'Ok, in that case, none of the boys in the school will be allowed out to play until the boys who climbed over the car confess. I will also cancel tonight's football match.'

At last two boys stood up at the back.

'I did it, sir.'

'I did it, sir.'

Then, like a scene from *Spartacus*, one boy after another stood up and said it was them.

Eventually every boy in the school was standing, from the big bruisers in Year 6 to the little tots in Year 1 who didn't have a clue what was happening. To give credit to Ed, he dismissed them all and later laughed like a kookaburra.

The ripples on the swimming pool begin to fade and once more I am back in the present. Over the blue divide I see a grey haired portly man leading his brood of ducklings. It looks like - it can't be - no.

Yes…it is! It's cynical Ed. He waves and grins and obviously still recognises me. Maybe I haven't changed as much as him.

Back to the coach and a quick dab at numeracy before lunch, areas and perimeters. I play the role of a carpet shop owner and the kids play the role of new home owners. I make the part my own and consider that working in a carpet shop could be quite a cosy comfort if not for the dust mites. Being a village school, the year 5/6 classroom doubles as the school canteen, it is also the school office and the school gym. Meanwhile, the afternoon is taken up with school photographs, the arrival of the mobile library and Mrs. Groggin's black and white cat getting stuck up the belfry.

Date: Tuesday, 06.03.07
Location: South Terrace Community
Today's Enemy: School Architects

A now retired member of the Special Ace Supply once told me to beware of any school that incorporates the word 'community.' It's a big school in a tough part of town. The morning is bathed in sunlight but it's numbingly cold. I arrive early. So early that no one else is around. I have misjudged the traffic and so I sit at the piano in the school hall and play some Abba. Soon, a dapper little man pads across the shadows on the highly polished wooden floor and smiles approvingly. Perhaps *The Winner Takes It All* reminds him of his youthful midnight fantasies over the blonde one.

'I'll give you Year 6,' he says, 'I don't want to be sexist but they are unsettled and may respond better to a man.'

When I was in my first year of teaching an ancient, gnarled, thumbless metalwork teacher growled, 'let me give you some advice son, kids are like dogs.' At the time, I was affronted by his seeming lack of political correctness but now I think he had a point. Kids are like dogs, they have a pack mentality and can smell fear, but after teaching Year 11s in Leeds there is not a whiff of fear about me when I teach Year 6 kids.

However, rule number 5 is to never be complacent. I once taught in a primary school in Leeds. Some of those kids would have scared the shit out of Attila the Hun. Apart from behavioural difficulties, the other big problem at that school was the heat. The classrooms were all south facing and the sun would hammer down on the huge plate glass windows. In summer it brought you to your knees and all you wanted to do at the end of the day was to throw yourself off a sand dune and roll down it, over and over, straight into a gushing pool of Stella Artois. I reckon architects who design schools are sadistic, revengeful bastards.

At break time I meet up with my pilot chum again who is complaining about the hours. All schools are different. This school works from 8.45 to 11.10 without a break. There is no afternoon break either when the sun is at its zenith. He describes it as a long haul flight and we laugh but only because we don't cry.

During afternoon assembly, the Head gives a dour speech about suicides that have been caused through bullying. It's a sensitive issue and one I have experienced both as a child and an adult. On both occasions, the bullies backed off when I finally found the courage to confront them, but that is not always an option for a child. At the end of the day the kids thank me and ask if I will come back again. It's a good sign and praise enough. The plane is safely landed, the passengers are happy and I'm heading home.

Date: Wednesday, 07.03.07
Location: St. Boswells
Today's Enemy: Coats

Strange. My muscles twitch in expectation of a good work out. My body is priming itself like a kid looking forward to a caravan holiday. Now there's an idea, a weekend in a caravan sitting in the middle of a field, preferably on a rainy day with a nice bottle of red and a good read.

I have a grim journey to work after a spat with my eldest son over the forgetting of coats. My eldest son might as well transfer his wardrobe to his classroom. The latest fad is for V neck jumpers to be worn off the shoulder. Was I that desperate to be an individual at eleven? Hell yeah. I used to weep when my mother forced me to get my hair cut back in the mop top era.

My hopes of a workout are quashed when, for the second time in three weeks, Declan decides not to bother turning up. I could take it personally but I refuse to. So now it's a days cover in Grimsville, Hellstown. I am to teach maths and they lead me by the nose to the maths block. The classroom is a shithole. The teacher, whoever he or she is, has obviously given up, poor bastard.

The view from the second floor classroom would be pleasant on a good day but today portentous clouds hang in the sky like ugly predators and the wind howls like an addicted wolf too long after its last shot of heroin. The Head of Department shows me the timetable and apologises for the fact that all of the classes are bottom sets. God help the teacher who usually takes them, they must have been a right bastard in their last life.

The first class arrive, a Year 9 in a huddle. I have decided that from now on I will never lose my temper. I will not even raise my voice because that is the trigger for the brain to flood the engine. I must endeavour never to lose it because, once lost, it cannot be regained until the superfluous petrol has dried out. Halfway through the lesson there are several bush fires erupting which I put out calmly and whenever the action goes hyper I deliberately slow my actions and speech to counter it.

'You sound like the Terminator, sir,' says one youth rocking back on his chair.

Today, the Terminator is garrulous in comparison.

The head of department comes in at the beginning of each lesson and sets the work, usually old exam papers.

'I could have been an actuary,' she whispers.

During another lesson, a huge boy asks the class, for reasons unknown, to put their hands up if they live with both parents. I decide to let his research continue unabated as I am intrigued. It turns out that out of a class of twenty six there is only one boy living with both parents and I am reminded that my wife and I split up five years ago when the boys were seven and six.

At lunchtime, I go to the staff room and immediately fall asleep for a full thirty minutes. I am shaken from my slumbers by the sound of a piercing siren which is the school's innovative way of making sure the kids don't linger outside.

The last lesson is the bottom set of a Year 11. They are bloody big and their mood, along with the wind and weather, is pug ugly. They receive yet another tired old exam paper but they prefer to twang rulers and make suggestive remarks to the three girls who give a whole lot better than they get to the point where the boys are forced to clam up in embarrassment after several references to their impoverished performances and penis size.

The final siren and I am out of there in the beamer with that big white prow cutting a swathe through the tempestuous navy blue.

```
Date: Thursday, 08.03.07
Location: Caius College, Radford
Today's Enemy: Anarchy
```

My regular Thursday teaching at St. Boswells is cancelled due to the school having a training day. I remember training days with warmth. It was a time when the wheel slowed down for a few hours and we could do adult things like go to the pub for lunch. The trade-off was to be subjected to the latest educational directives that had drifted down the Virginia creeper of an Oxbridge college.

Personally, I prefer to teach, even if it is in Radford. Did I say Radford? Under normal circumstances, I would have rolled about on the floor squealing with a mixture of mirth and alarm at the merest mention of Radford. Once bitten, twice pathologically retiring. However, I am an elite member of the SAS and my impulsive gung ho spirit and war correspondent machismo mean I say 'yes', much to the Agency's surprise.

The grandiloquently named Caius College is a fine example of early Victorian architecture but the exterior is purely cosmetic for within the well-dressed walls there grows a consuming melanoma. Fear and dread drip down the flaking walls and this is going to be one mother of a mission. I walk down a dark inhospitable corridor searching for reception, mentally unravelling a ball of string as I go.

'Can I help you?'

I jump.

'I'm the Headmaster.'

A bucolic man in his late fifties stares up at me, bloodshot of eye, purple of nose and high of blood pressure. Fluffy white hair and a crumpled grey suit, all the colour washed out of him. He reports that ten regulars have phoned in sick. I ask in pretend innocence if there is something going around.

'No,' he answers, checking his watch. 'Ten is normal. If it wasn't for people like you, the school would close.'

Somehow his comment feels more like chastisement than praise. I am to teach science and the fast fading Headmaster asks a passing teacher to show me to Dr. Frankenstein's laboratory. As we progress down a few miles of begrimed passageway, I cannot help but notice gaping holes smashed into the ceiling at regular intervals. I query my guide, a young man with Rastafarian ringlets, as to their significance.

'They smash in the panels with chairs,' he says grinning and carries on whistling *Buffalo Soldiers*. We pass a smashed drinks machine and climb two flights of stairs, which he takes three at a time. At the top we turn left down another corridor, which disappears up its own one point perspective before finally stopping at a reinforced steel door.

'Good luck,' he says shaking my hand and smiling.

'Good luck,' he calls again from the shadows. Suddenly there is a terrific clap of thunder and a flash of lightning.

This is going to be tough. I may have made a mistake. I could lose it and then I will be suspended without the comfort of pay. In the police they call it 'gardening time.' The laboratory is devoid of apparatus. The cinematic image of bubbling conical flasks will not happen here. The glassware probably had the same fate as the ceiling panels. The layout of the lab is familiar, scratched hardwood desks, gas taps - not working - I check. Ceramic sinks, narrow nozzled taps for filling non-existent test tubes, empty glass cabinets with cracked glass panes and tall wooden stools.

8.50am. Ten minutes to go and I can hear the adrenalin slopping around the sluice gates of my stomach. My mind goes back to Grammar school when I sat with aching bum cheeks on the knotted pine, frowning as the alchemist filled the board with numbers and letters and somehow made them all fit together while my brain became a milky mixture. Three minutes to go and it suddenly occurs to me that no work has been set. A practical experiment is out, even if there was any equipment, so I find a heap of ragged textbooks and a chapter on the properties of metal.

9.00am and I hear the sound of thunder again created by a hellish banging on the steel doors. Against all instincts of survival, I open it and the kids that enter look feral. Twelve boys and seven girls and the hostility is palpable. This is bloody dangerous and my atavistic intuitions are honed. They rock on their stools and finger-drum the tables and generally try to out gross each other. I ask a boy with SS insignia cut into his skinhead haircut if he will hand out the exercise books. He takes the pile of books. He gives a snaggle toothed grin and promptly drops them into a sink half full of water (or should that be half empty?)

He then retrieves the books but only to launch them across the room. The rest of the class catch them and either redirect them at someone else or Frisbee them out of the window. Next, they attach hosepipes to the taps and soak each other with high-pressure jets and they are as wild eyed as mountain cats. This isn't beating out bush fires, this is a full forest inferno and I have a leaky bucket. They start to walk out of the lab but I block them and ask in growing bewilderment where they think they are going. They look shocked as if it's the first time their actions have been questioned.

'Get out of the fucking way, science is boring,' rasps a girl with a big broken nose.

'Science is boring.' Discuss, making reference to the work of Archimedes, Copernicus, Hypocrites, Marconi, Turin, Caxton, Descartes, Galileo, Rutherford, Bell, Curie, Jenner, Fleming, Boyle, Edison, Watt, Mendel, Einstein, Newton, Diesel, Darwin, Hawkin, Crick and Watson.

I'll lose it if I shout but I have no choice.

'Sit down! You are not leaving this room until the lesson is finished.'

The girl with the nose rushes towards me and screams in my face, 'Fuck off, you cunt!'

I shout louder, 'Sit down! You are not going anywhere.'

She screams even louder and pierces my eardrum and I am just inhaling a huge draught of air ready to crack the remaining teat pipette when she slaps me in the face. It does the trick. I calm down and leave for assistance.

'Who is it?' Snaps the Headmaster, responding to the urgent knocking on his door.

I explain through the door and begrudgingly he appears. 'Here,' he says proffering a key, 'get back in there, and this time lock the bloody door so they can't get out!'

I laugh as I am prone to do in moments of hysteria. I suggest he should speak to the class as the situation is past critical.

'Shut up!' he shrieks, only just falling short of calling me a snivelling, lily-livered coward and I retreat before receiving my second slap of the morning on the tail end of a 'for God's sake man, pull yourself together!'

I've had enough. I desert my post, but not before advising the Caretaker to turn the water and gas off at the mains. Anarchy rules ok.

Date: Friday, 09.03.02
Location: St. Boswells
Today's Enemy: Scantily-clad ladies

After Radford, St. Boswells is like a cosy café with a log fire and inglenooks. Lo! Is that a scatter cushion in the alcove and a *Horse and Hound* magazine? A pot of Darjeeling from the foothills of the Himalayas, if you please, and a slice of walnut cake, if you will.

A startling realisation. Somewhere there is a school that is worse than Caius College and somewhere else there is a school that is worse than that.

The boys from Year 10. I love the smell of armpits in the morning. I have purchased, out of my own funds, several motorbike magazines which I distribute. The conceit being that the boys choose a motorbike and create an information sheet about it. They flick through the mags and the images arrest their attention immediately. Yes, it has worked. At last, I have found something they are interested in. I am too cunning for them.

'Look at the tits on her!' Exclaims the foul Darren.

'They're massive!' Adjoins the rotting Billy.

Damn. In my innocence, I have neglected to consider the connection between fast bikes and faster women, breasts and buttocks. Firm Kawasaki straddling thighs are everywhere. Even an advert for a sump oil container is modelled by a silicon lipped, bare arsed beauty. I gather them in and do a quick censorship job on them which results in the bulk of the magazines being tossed in the bin.

Later the boys relay to me that they had a 'posh cunt' teaching them yesterday.

I question their language.

'You are just like him,' says Darren, 'correcting us every time we speak.'

I want to explain the difference between someone who asks them to curtail the 'C' word and someone who complains about their stopped glottals like some loopy latter day Henry Higgins, but I don't.

'He said we were all twats, sir, who would end up in jail and that he was leaving and would never return.'

'Did he say he was going to Spain?'

'Eh?'

'Never mind.'

I recall the same teacher sitting in the staffroom one day last week emitting loud bothersome coughs every few seconds as if to say, 'Help me, please. For God's sake help me, I'm being torn asunder.'

There was nothing I could do for him. You make your own choices in life.

In addition to the magazines I have also bought a sack of stationery. These boys have never brought a pencil to class, so I lend them pencils which are never returned and do not make it to their next classroom. Where do they go?

The new pencils have no points on them so I sharpen them with a Stanley knife over the bin. Behind me, I hear loud guffaws but I finish sharpening the pencils anyway, then a boy asks if I can sharpen his pencil too. I turn my back again and the guffaws get louder. Then a girl asks me, between giggles, if I can sharpen hers too. I turn again and the guffaws are heading into the next phase of unsuppressed laughter. I am intrigued but continue to switch the blunt Stanley knife across the pencil, feeling my arse wobble with the effort. The recently acquired M&S stretch cords I am wearing are just going with the flow and I realise now what the joke is. I turn round and there are four more of the swine lining up with pencils. They see the smile in my eyes and maybe for the first time with this class it's not another 'me and them' situation but all of us enjoying the joke together.

At lunchtime, I go to the staff room and drift off to the sound of four large women discussing their prospective pensions.

'If I leave now, at fifty eight, I will receive £4,500 pounds a year.'

I consider as I go into beta sleep that £90 a week will not even pay her weekly cake bill.

The last lesson of the week is a potentially troublesome Year 7 that have given me pound for pound the hardest time of all. Recently, they have been fine but only because ten of the most wearisome disappear off the radar screen every Friday afternoon and I am not predisposed to sending out a stealth plane to find them, and no-one seems bothered, anyway.

**Date: The weekend
Location: Home
Enemy: Noisy Pubs**

I borrowed Fellini's *8½* from the school library, but in the words of Albert Steptoe, 'Eight and a half what?' We had better luck with *The Shipping News* starring Kevin Spacey, a good story with the bonus of a Newfoundland location. Later, we visited a city pub with friends but I couldn't hear a word anyone was saying because of the noise. There, I've said it. I'm old.

On Sunday I read *The Independent* and learn that one in four teenagers carries a knife and that there has been a 50% increase on attacks on teachers in the past year alone. The President of the NASUWT reports that, 'Teaching is terrifying!'

Date: Monday, 12.03.07
Location: St. Boswells
Today's Enemy: *Groundhog Day*

I wait an hour for a class to arrive due to the entire school being in some mega assembly. This provides the time to calculate that during that hour I have earned fifty million Turkish lira. Today I am to cover for the drama teacher. No! Not drama, please. Already, I can hear the sound of revving chairs. The unfortunate that normally teaches drama is still around but can hardly talk and looks like Banquo's ghost. He wants me to show *Groundhog Day* to three different groups throughout the day.

'Is that the movie where a man is trapped in the same place doing the same thing every day and feeling that everything he does is worthless?'

'The very same.'

'Ah.'

As expected, the drama studio is another aircraft hangar and as cold as a penguin's piles due to the cloud level ceiling. Thirty kids, dressed in cotton shirts, will endure extreme temperatures while they watch a film about a weatherman. I hunt down another member of the department who cranks a red lever and the heaters kick in. Fine, apart from the accompanying noise which turns the drama studio into the launch pad at Cape Canaveral. The speakers on the TV rattle and crackle as they try to make themselves audible above the sound of fifty screaming rocket engines but, as with almost any flickering cathode ray, the film somehow holds their attention.

After lunch I watch *Groundhog Day* again. This time I know most of what is coming. I say 'most' because, to my concern, I see and hear bits that I must have missed the first time which was just over an hour ago. This makes me wonder just how much or maybe how little of reality I actually perceive. Maybe I'm being too selective. If so, and I am selecting only the good bits of a day, then just how bad is this place?

It's parent's evening at my youngest son's primary school and I can't wait to bask in his teachers' praises. It's been the same since nursery and tonight is no different.

'A joy to teach.'

'Excellent in all subjects.'

'The problem will be choosing which direction he wants to go in.'

'Perhaps there is a job where he can use all his talents.'

He's thinking primary school teacher and his teacher promises that he will try to talk him out of it.

Date: Tuesday, 13.03.07
Location: Carlow Village Primary School
Today's Enemy: The unknown

It's my first visit to this one and also a first for the Agency.
'We are sending you as our ambassador,' they tell me.
Very nice, but what about a little extra in the old pay poke for all this ambassadorial work? The school is a little grey stone building tucked in behind four rows of Victorian terraces and an offy. The kids wear royal blue tops with a school logo and look very neat. I am introduced to the Headmistress and we exchange knowing grins as I once worked with her in a school situated in one of the roughest council estates in Leeds where half of the houses had their windows filled in with bricks like latter day glass tax avoiders.

That school was at the end of a cul-de-sac of such houses and I felt like I was running a gauntlet every day. I remember on one occasion we were taking the kids on a school trip but the coach couldn't negotiate the gauntlet so we had to walk them from the school to the end of the road. It was a scorcher of a day and when we returned in the afternoon the front gardens were full of mothers dancing in bra and knickers, windows open and speakers blasting out music by Status Quo, each clutching a bottle of wine in one hand and a fag in the other and shouting, 'Hi, Kylie love. Fish and chips for tea if you go get 'em.'

The teachers worked hard at that school and I salute them for dealing with the constant flow of shit that that they wiped up everyday. Unfortunately, the Headmaster was a ruthless ambitious bastard who didn't give four pence for the welfare of his staff. Most were unhappy and several had nervous breakdowns. One class I taught was fine apart from two 11 year old girls who were psychopaths, and I don't use the term lightly. I removed them after one tried to stab the other in the eye with a freshly sharpened 2HB pencil only to have them returned five minutes later by the rising star Headmaster holding one in each hand. The term ferrets in a rabbit hutch never rang more true.

Five minutes later, after extracting their hands one finger at a time from a little girl's throat I returned them to the rising star who promptly returned them to sender. Anyone for tennis?

Julie was the Deputy Head and I used to deliberate just how come a statuesque, upper middle class, piano playing, opera singing blonde was here in downtown Leeds and not running her own International Glamour Company from her Paris HQ. I was there for one term and during it I hardly moved out of the staff room. Instead, I used to read and write poetry and drink cups of tea and read the obscure literature that some agent would plonk on the staff room table; cook books, D.I.Y., Beatrix Potter's diaries, gardening books, alongside cushions stuffed with violets, singing Billy the bass fish, x-ray specs, beardie dries, abdominal muscle developers, vacuum pumps, arc lamps, lawn aeriating shoes, singing ringing trees and all the other detritus that is somehow associated with primary school teachers.

I was never asked to teach. It was incredible, a most unique situation, a bit like being a grounded spitfire pilot waiting for the scramble bell that never rang. I never questioned it, then one day I was called into the rising star's office to be told that another position had been found for me at a different aerodrome. I was well miffed because I was halfway through writing a novel, developing a six pack and learning how to bake the perfect scone.

So now Julie has her own modest school in a tidy little village and all those years in the wilderness have paid off. We kept our past lives to a cursory greeting and I was shown my class.

Year 1. No work has been set and the flight plan reads 'Do whatever you please!' This class comes with a support teacher because one of the boys is on drugs to keep him off the ceiling. It's a drug they give to kids who will not acquiesce gracefully to sitting in a box all day.

A good classroom assistant is priceless: they are a contact with the adult world, for being in a box with 30 six-year-olds is not the most cerebral experience. Indeed, teaching can be a very lonely job, especially as a supply teacher where relationships with the rest of the staff are often kept to 'there is paper in that drawer', 'don't use the red mug' and 'it's your duty.' I also have the indispensable Gordon the green guitar with me so I should just about survive. The theme for the day will be pirates. The support teacher, a lovely lady known as Auntie Tina, is even more enthusiastic than the kids and finds five giant cardboard boxes which we reassemble into the hull of *The Black Pig*. Long cardboard tubes, the middles of carpet rolls, provide a mast, a telescope, several cannons and the bow sprit. A large sheet makes a sail and a flag is made from a quickly drawn skull and crossbones on a piece of black satin.

'I'm enjoying this,' says a smiling Tina. 'Their usual teacher is really old and she can hardly get out of the chair.'

The bug eyed five and six-year-olds enter the room and go ohhhh! and ahhhh! Their imagination is launched and we sing drunken sailors' shanties, dance a crazy jig, look at grid references on a treasure map, write a little play, draw pirate ships and tell pirate stories and at the end of the day I sling my hook and leave the lovely Tina waving a lacy 'kerchief at the quayside.

Date: Wednesday, 14.03.07
Location: St Gregorian's Primary
Today's Enemy: The Snow Queen

This used to be one of my regular schools. I have taught whole terms at this place, had some of my greatest moments there, including the 'Circus.' However, it is five years since my last appearance as Ringmaster. I remember it as a happy school but with the potential to disappear up its own arse. The reason it didn't was due to one woman, the one and only Pauline, a chain-smoking Geordie marvel in her mid-fifties with a voice as smoky as a New Orleans jazz club and the ability to put the whole crazy world of education into perspective with just one dirty music hall chortle. Her laughter was infectious to pandemic proportions. I have witnessed a succession of Headteachers nervously shuffle the latest government doctrines back into their newly acquired leather look attaché cases after being hit with a well aimed snort that projected scorn, contempt, ridicule and transcendent intelligence all at once. Similarly, any back biting was treated with a similar response until the biter felt bitten. She was the hub of a wheel and one of the few that continued to fly over the cuckoo's nest. When a new neurotic Headmistress arrived, it was the final straw for Pauline and she took early retirement. In her words, 'we had a big top here once but now it's just a house of misery.'

There were four new teachers, all young women and every one of them looked cowed, all victims of the Snow Queen who made her first appearance during morning assembly, entering in theatrical style through the curtains and onto the stage of the Royal Adelphi. A woman in her extremely late forties who was always power dressed and had enormous, incongruous breasts that should have been attached to a giving earth mother. I listened as she dictated her latest diatribe to the innocent and naïve before disappearing for the rest of the week to attend a course on man management.

Year 5 were described as a 'lively bunch' which is another educational euphemism along the lines of 'challenging behaviour', 'bit of a character' and 'long term illness.' I think the reason some kids 'try it on' with a new teacher is because they are on such a tight reign with their usual one. Children, being only semi-trained, will break loose and make for the wide open plains at the drop of a halter. To make my life easier, and believe me that's all I am concerned about, I tend to go with the flow in these situations. Classes that have a rigid teacher tend to be the afore-mentioned one trick ponies who can only respond to their usual trainer.

With this garnered knowledge, I quickly abandon any attempt to teach a formal curriculum and pull out a few 'specials.' It's my mantra that teaching is all about survival and most Headteachers are quite content for the class to be out of their hair for the day - unless they are the Snow Queen, who insisted on making an appearance every fifteen minutes to check we weren't knotting sheets together.

At lunchtime, I went to a staff room that once resonated to the sound of laughter only to find it empty.

During afternoon registration one of the kids, an Asian girl, told me that she liked to watch Bollywood films and then copy all the dances.

'You mean Hollywood,' said her freckle faced chum.

'No, I do not,' said the exasperated Asian girl rolling her big brown eyes in true Bollywood style.

'I can do the dances if you like,' she said, clapping her hands, 'I have my special clothes in my bag and a tape of the music.'

Gooooooooo with the flooooooooooow.

For the next ten minutes, she delighted and enchanted the

entire class who had never seen anything like it. Afterwards I told her that it was absolutely incredible, a feast of sound and vision and I couldn't believe that her classmates had never seen her dancing before. In fact, I was so inspired by her dancing that I wanted everyone in the entire school to feel the same. In the days of Pauline it would have been a case of nipping down to her class and saying, 'stop everything, I'm sending a dancer down,' and Pauline would have said, 'oh, yes please.' The little Asian girl was more than happy to dance for the whole school, this was her fairytale moment, her big chance. At break time I gushed with enthusiasm and asked the other teachers if they would like their class to enjoy some amazing dancing and music from another culture, complete with gold lame costume and red slippers.

'No,' they said. 'She wouldn't like it.'

Suddenly I am McMurphy, flying over the cuckoo's nest, 'but it's the big game! C'mon, you guys you wanna watch the World Series don'tcha? C'mon, you're kidding me, the World Series, you know what I'm saying here? An Asian girl dancing in true Bollywood tradition with all the movements and gestures to a tape of tabla and harmonium and wearing full traditional costume. C'mon now, get your freaking hands in the air!'

At the end of the day I was informed by the secretary that my proposed return the following week had been cancelled. Ah well, at least I got to keep my frontal lobes.

Date: Thursday, 15.03.07
Location: Diggon Local Primary
Today's Enemy: St. Boswells

I have told the agency that deals with St. Boswells that I'm ill. I am lying in a muddy, lice infested, fox hole with my eyes wide open pretending to be dead as the enemy moves over and on. Someone else must do the fighting for a while - Prince Andrew, Prince Michael of Kent, Prince Harry - I don't care who.

I contact a different agency and they dispatch me to a local primary. The school is in a leafy suburb but that means nothing, many of the houses are rented out to single teenage mothers. This will be a foot stuck on the accelerator day with no chance for a sandwich in the slow lane. The kids are wary of me at first, they put feelers out, they have their methods, an almost imperceptible whisper, no response, a nudge, a raised voice, still no response, a shove, a push, a slap, more voices joining in.

'If I point to you, don't worry, it just means that you stay in at break and write me a two page letter of apology.'

Silence.

The Headmistress waddles in and introduces herself. She has spiky yellow hair and bee stung lips and I am reminded of a very large and wonderful duck.

'You'll have no problem with this class,' she says, 'but when you do, send them to me.'

The morning passes uneventfully and the kids begin to relax and converse. Unfortunately, the stories they tell are horror stories concerning attempted abductions, thumped mothers, burglaries and their own cigarette addiction.

'Please,' I beg, 'no more, enough.'

SAS: Supply Ace Special

I feel as though they are dragging me by the heels into a morass of deprivation.

At lunch I drive as far as I can within reason and quickly try to fall asleep to escape their demons. The afternoon is booked for PE and so I put them into four teams and we play six-a-side football. After five minutes, I have to abandon the session because there would be more sporting goodwill between England and Argentina in a game played on the Falklands circa 1982. I have never experienced as much bad feeling, angst, aggression, animosity and general dumping of frustration than I encountered during that twenty minutes. The final casualty list was six girls in tears, one gasping for breath, three boys bleeding and another just plain disappeared. Never again. I open and close my account on that one. Too risky.

Date: Friday, 16.03.07
Location: Parland Green Primary
Today's Enemy: Horror Stories and Demons

Another first and I pray it will go better than yesterday's debacle. Supply teaching could be the perfect job for the travelling spirit, the onion man attempting to be rid of the choking layers of indoctrination. There is a school in almost every village of this large island so it would not be totally unfeasible to hitch up a caravan and tour it in the style of a Daniel Defoe or a Dr. Johnson and spend, say, half a term in Cornwall followed by half a term in Devon and ending up forty years later doing a stint at the Kyle of Lochalsh Comprehensive teaching RE instead of being incarcerated in the same tiny cell for a quadruple life sentence. Even the bird man of Alcatraz found peace and inner content.

Normally, I would be at St. Boswells but I find Fridays there physically gruelling, psychologically damaging and spiritually disengaging. This is due in part to the double lesson when I attempt to teach *Macbeth* to 9X. It's a case of hubble bubble double trouble, where the clock hands defy physics and spin backwards until I am tumbling through time to teach their stone age ancestors who, like their progeny, are more interested in clubbing than learning.

So today I opt instead for a Year 5 in a village primary school. On the way I listen to the news - London teachers are striking today because they can't afford to teach and live in a house at the same time. There is also an item about a school in

Northumberland that is teaching the Creationist view of human existence, which insists that nothing is older than six thousand years and that the world was indeed created in seven days. What's the difference? The Creationist hypothesis is just the theory of Evolution on speed.

I arrive at the school. A sixties building surrounded, like most State schools, by a few grotty thirty-year-old 'temporary measure' portacabins. The schools, Heads, secretaries, teachers and kids have finally become one amorphous mass with one thousand heads, four thousand limbs and a million eyes. The Headmaster takes me to a particularly shabby looking example of a portacabin, which is full of badgers, cats, squirrels and owls but I am no longer fazed by the strange. They are not real, just the after-effect of a tall glass of mescal I drank last night. The class have arrived early to prepare for their first performance of *Puss in Boots*. It's panto time and I'm getting paid to watch. My first reaction is one of pleasure, but after a few minutes of squeals and shrieks of hysteria I change my mind.

The panto is well received. The teacher on the battered piano is excellent, the singing is great and the acting is beautifully wooden, apart from the leather booted Puss who has a certain panache. On this occasion, his Sylvester-esque speech impediment works to his advantage. Afterwards, I congratulate the pianist and she thanks me and tells of her early days playing jazz on sea-cruises with a twenty-five stone black drummer from Memphis. She also converses in ever shifting tangents and can swing from a cramped shared cabin with a hairdresser to her drooling admiration for dark haired men with designer stubble at the twitch of a panto cat's tail.

Even more intriguing than the jazz player was a teaching assistant who relayed a series of gory stories from her paramedic husband.

'Last week,' she said taking a quick slurp of tea, 'he was sent to recover a twenty stone lorry driver. The driver had parked next to a length of embedded scaffold tubing and when he jumped out of his cab...well it was dark, you see, and...jam doughnut, anyone? ... Yesterday, he was called out to a suicide case where a man had jumped off a bridge and somehow landed vertically which sent his thigh bones careering through his torso thereby depositing his cock and balls on top of his head...pass the ketchup, please.'

The weather is evil, a bitter and twisted east wind firing sleet darts and ice bullets but this school centres on the ethos of Sparta and the kids are made to go outside at break. Unfortunately, so am I and I close my eyes and think of Tahiti. The other duty teacher has fifteen semi-frozen kids hanging off her coat. It emerges that she's from the U.S.A. and her accent breaks the nightmare I had last night when I was part of a crowd looking up at a star spangled tank listening to a gum chewing soldier telling us that the big boys were here now and that we should all chant 'Long live President Bush.'

After lunch, the class design a recycling poster employing the Admans' rule of three; Re-use, Recycle, Reduce. At 3.20, I am Re-leased. As I drive home, a programme on the radio is dealing with the concept of infinity and whether it is possible to have infinity plus one. They discuss 'Hibble's Hotel', which has an infinite number of rooms, all of which are full until a weary traveller arrives and desperately needs one. To oblige him, the owner asks all his residents to move out of their room and go into the room next door, hence the traveller can now stay in room number one. The hotel wasn't full after all. Later, a coach arrives with an infinite number of passengers who all want an infinite number of rooms in the infinitely roomed Hotel. The owner has a solution, he asks everyone to move to the room that is double the number of the room they are already in, so one goes to two, two to four, three to six, four to eight, five to ten and so on. Consequently, room number one is now empty and so is room number three, room number five and every other odd number for infinity. So the hotel with the infinite number of rooms that was considered full has found rooms for an infinite number of coach passengers, badgers, squirrels, owls, jazz pianists, paramedics, twenty-five stone black drummers, American tank soldiers and sibilant pantomime cats. Of course, the reality is that the hotel manager would slam the door shut on a poor and weary traveller when the hotel was full the first time.

Date: Weekend
Location: Castle Howard
Today's Enemy: Crows and Cages

A friend, Tony, is staying for the weekend. A singular man, aged sixty. His needs are minimal, a bottle or two of averagely priced claret every day and a weekly visit to the theatre. He has managed to avoid work for the past twenty years and so effectively retired at forty. He lives in a neat council high-rise and last month, because he reached sixty, he no longer has to sign on, an act he bitterly resented and feared. He is now liberated and, though he has no material wealth, he has the health and attitude of a man who hasn't spent his early middle age in shackles.

I take him walking to the country side around Castle Howard to see a wood famous for its deep pile carpets of bluebells. We walk to the pyramid folly and then head in the direction of the flowers, but stop halfway. Two crows have been trapped in two of four compartments of a simple stick and spring cage and are furiously pecking at the chicken wire and flapping their ragged wings in confusion. Periodically, they pace the restricted area before pecking and scratching at the wire again. It is dreadful to witness. We stand as still as the Castle Howard statues, minds flailing over the ethics.

For me, the symbolism is only too apparent, a trapped creature denied the freedom of the skies by the width of a wire. I am minded to free them but Tony advises against interfering and suggests that crows have a reputation for pecking out the eyes of lambs. I suggest that these particular crows may not be guilty of causing the lambs to scream but are being punished for their kind. He agrees, but insists we should not meddle. It's a cruel fate for the crows in the prime of their being to be caged in such a manner.

I desperately want to release them so I reach my hand into one of the empty compartments to inspect the holding mechanism. The movement causes the trap to spring again, pinning my arm against the internal wire and making the crow on the other side angry. It stabs at my hand with its cruel beak five, six times and I feel it drilling against my bones. I feel nauseous and shout for Tony to try and ease back the strong steel spring, it's an awkward bastard though, quite devilish and the lid resists as the crow in a growing frenzy pecks faster and harder at my now bleeding hand. Unable to find the science, Tony upends the crow cage to try and keep the crow at the bottom but this only makes it more angry and I feel its beak vibrating through my entire skeleton. Tony is pulling with both hands and I use my free hand and we yank and tug until finally it gives and I am freed but shaking. I hold no malice towards the crows but there is no more I can do.

I tried but it wasn't to be.

Date: Monday, 19.03.07
Location: Horton Village Primary
Today's Enemy: Enemy Vomit

Another first for me: a school high on the wild moors. If this was Australia, I would have to fly there. It's a four hour round trip but I take it purely out of intrigue. I leave at 6am and head north until I am surrounded by purple gorse and world weary sheep. This is untamed, barren country, a man could die up here if he should stray off the track but today the weather is benign and it's a pleasure to be up on what feels like the very roof of England.

A couple of miles further brings me into the village and I see the grey stone and black slate school. It's small, but the playground is tiny which is mad as the building is surrounded by wilderness. I park outside and a woman, who I correctly surmise to be the Head, greets me at the door. She's mid-fifties with a brillo-pad haircut in the style of a helmet, pouchy cheeks, dark ringed eyes, cardigan, shirt, desert boots, and she stands with her fingers tucked into her trouser pockets, thumbs exposed.

'Morning,' she calls, 'you must be the supply. How are you?'

I'm tempted to shout, 'fair dinkum' as I manoeuvre the chocs under the wheels of my Cessna two seater plane.

'Fine, thanks.'

'Where have you come from?'

'Station 45. Now what's all this about a sick joey?'

She shows me round the school which takes less than a minute and then begins her tirade against the education authority.

'A couple of years ago I asked them to build us a modern toilet block so they came and nailed plastic corrugated sheets across the outbuilding. There's no heat either. In winter we freeze our you-know-what's off.'

I would have responded with some placatory remark just to be polite but there was really no need; I was a sounding board and my purpose was to listen until her spleen was double vented.

'Rats,' she hissed, prolonging the hiss for nape of neck hair crawling effect. 'Rats, I've seen them with my own two eyes, right there, scurrying across the floor bold as brass. I don't mind spiders or even a mouse but not ratsssss.'

I was shown to one of two tiny class rooms.

'You take the young ones, she said, 'and I'll take the older ones because it's sex week. Ssssssssex education. I don't mind what you teach them as long as its reading, writing and numbers.'

The kids began to arrive, just a few solitary lost sheep at first then a herd as the old cowshit splattered Landrovers poured out their 'cooked breakfast every morning' progeny. There were thirty in the class all crammed into the small room like refugee sardines in a smuggler's tin. It was a similar situation in the little square playground but still they managed, through advanced sonar techniques, to play four separate games of football, three games of tig and a skipping game with a rope that was the length of the diagonal.

Then it began.

I was crouching down to help a boy draw a figure five, trying to overcome the pain of arthritis in my knees, when without even a two second warning, he threw up that morning's full English into my face which sent me reeling backwards with the shock and dumped me in an incredulous heap on the dusty wooden floor. He wasn't finished though because he threw back his head and released a jet of vomit that made Linda Blair's attempt in *The Exorcist* look like an innocuous piece of spinach trapped between her teeth. The multicoloured discharge rained down on me and spattered across the floor.

Worse was to come.

The little girl who had been sitting next to him and who probably didn't have a strong stomach at the best of times somehow managed to stand up and rush over to where I was lying before dropping her load over my churning stomach. I tried to stand up, but the action of placing my flat hand in a freshly regurgitated pile of eggy bacon bits caused me to recoil and slip on the sticky stuff and down I went again.

Yet worse was to come because whatever it was that their little stomachs were so forcefully rejecting, it didn't mind which route it took - either the high road or the low road, it was all the same. Out of the thirty kids in the class, only two refrained from hoying their kippers.

It was the same in the other class too, kids were spewing up everywhere and the be-cardiganned head skidded, skated and slid across the floor to the telephone to get the old shit splattered Landrovers back pronto to take their little pukers home, leaving me wondering how I had suddenly become a Jackson Pollock exhibit. It was still only 10am and the school was now empty, apart from the Head, myself, and twenty five gallons of grunge.

'It looks like we won't be needing you after all,' said the desert booted lady, fingers entrenched in her pockets and thumbs jerking like two pinball flippers. 'Sorry about that. I hope it hasn't been a wasted journey.'

I smiled and promptly threw up every morsel of food I have ever eaten in the past fifteen years, even that troublesome piece of smoked German sausage that had been trapped between the colon and the small intestine since the 1980 Munich beer festival.

As an addendum to this, the outbreak of the virus made the national news and the school was closed for a week for steam cleaning. No doubt the kids were fine the following day whereas I didn't receive a penny for my input, not even a little something for the laundry bill. Ratssss.

Date: Tuesday, 20.03.07
Location: Banfield/Millham
Today's Enemy: Data Collecting & Frequency Tables

A double; two schools in one day. First, Banfield Catholic school in the morning, followed by Millham Primary in the afternoon. I would like to make a good first impression at Banfield, so I wear a dark suit and tie. I want to make a good impression because it is a handy school and I am fed up of sitting in traffic jams on the way to Leeds. Also, I am pissed off with begrudging attitudes. The St. Boswell kids make no secret of the fact that school bores them rigid. As the boy Declan said, 'What use is history to me?' It's true, let's admit it, these kids need a trade, plumbers are the new barristers, they need to be taught life skills, how to get a mortgage, how to change a nappy, how to make a million out of property and the stock market, how to play the game and not be wage slaves for the rest of their lives.

It's a sunny morning at Banfield and I'm early so I make a call on the mobile to talk to Margaret about nothing much at all. Our conversation is brought up short by the school caretaker tapping on the window.

'Are you lost?

'No, I'm teaching here this morning.'

'Oh,' he says looking at the beamer, the suit, and the mobile phone all at once.

'Nice car,' he says eventually.

'I was recently offered five hundred pounds for it,' I say.

'Never spoil an illusion,' he says, jabbing his finger on the bonnet. 'You don't look like a teacher.'

'What does a teacher look like?'

'Like him.'

The Headmaster resembled a *Thunderbirds* puppet with his snow white hair and black bushy eyebrows. Casually dressed in a sleeveless pullover and corduroy trousers, only a meerschaum pipe was missing and here's me in my dark suit, white beamer and chunky mobile phone. I mention that I was at his school recently watching my son's team playing football against his school.

'Ah yes, good game,' he mutters, then suddenly (and alarmingly) he raises those eyebrows and adds, 'you beat us one nil.'

'I know. My son scored the goal.'

The eyebrows arch violently and I am ready to drive away empty handed when he smiles and shakes my hand. 'It was a scorcher,' he said, 'I'll show you to the classroom.'

The room was spacious with good views of green fields and the big blue sky. Perfect apart from the bloody big crucifix on the wall. The Buddhists have a sweet rotund fellow with a gentle and benign smile and the Catholics have some poor sod with six inch nails hammered through his hands.

The work is already set, 'data collecting and frequency tables.' After break, they are to write a week's diary. To add spice, I ask them to write about a week where anything (and everything) could (and did!) happen. In true Catholic style, the results were as disturbing and alarming as the Head's eyebrows and ranged from the altar boy who crucified a pig to the girl who spent some time with her recently deceased dad, 'because when he was alive I never told him how much he meant to me.'

The afternoon school is only ten minutes away so I drive down to the river and watch it go by a while. Bliss, so much nicer than escaping into oblivion in that shit hole of a staff room at Leeds. After delaying as long as possible, I drive to Millham Primary, a matriarchy of a school favoured by new-age, trendy, middle-class, left-of-centre hippy types. Here, the boys have waist length hair and wear rainbow coloured pullovers and the girls affect a lisp. Actually, it's an interesting mix at this school which appears to have the Eastern philosophy of 'an ocean refuses no river.' The standards are high and the art work on display would do credit to the Tate Modern. By coincidence, I am asked to cover 'data gathering and frequency tables,' it must be that time of the academic year. It is said that whenever the Minister for Education looks at their watch they know exactly what every child will be studying at that time.

After break, it's PE and a meditation session. They can handle the esoteric here, it doesn't freak them out and soon the class are sleeping on the warm white sands of a tropical desert island until I bring them back to reality and a cold, hard gym floor. A couple of years ago I studied for a Diploma in Hypnotherapy and the first thing I learnt was how easy it is to hypnotise someone, the skill comes in knowing what to do when the person is hypnotised. The comments from children after relaxing and visualising are fabulous.

'I felt as though I was floating on a golden cloud.'

'It felt like I was riding on a dolphin's back over a rainbow.'

Sometimes the kids ask me to relax their mums and dads because they are always shouting at each other.

Last year I spent a week with the Year 6 kids from this school at an Outdoor Pursuits centre. It was in November and the worst week for rain on record. It didn't matter. We enjoyed being on the wild open moors instead of cooped up in a box. It was hard work though, often I didn't go to bed until after midnight through some kid crying for his mum. Strangely, it was always the little toughies who fared worse there. They don't do the trips anymore, fewer schools are willing to take the risk due to unnecessary lawsuits and unfortunate recent tragedies. It's a shame really as that week was a rite of passage for many.

Date: Wednesday, 21.03.07
Location: Blairtop
Today's Enemy: The Peacock

It could only happen at this school. They are spending the day having a full rehearsal for the Queen's birthday. The Headmistress, or the peacock as I call her, hands me a pile of paper plates with the instruction to get the class to decorate them in a manner befitting the occasion. We brainstorm the great events that have taken place during the Queen's reign and come up with England winning the World Cup in 1966.

With more effort, we manage the first moon landing, the conquering of Everest, the four minute mile, the birth of rock and roll, the Beatles, the white hot technological revolution of the Wilson Government and the hoolahoop. Most of the plates, however, simply feature the good old Union Jack and a crown with the words Happy, Birthday, Queen and Elizabeth written round the edges with infinite permutations and spellings. The peacock seemed happy enough. Next, she wanted me to change the words to *Jailhouse Rock* to 'something to do with the Queen' with the instructions to 'do it at lunchtime and we'll practise it this afternoon. Oh, and do the same for *Johnny B. Goode.*'

The words to *Jailhouse Rock* are actually fiendishly clever the way they scan to fit the rhythm, there is not a spare syllable. I give it a go and come up with a first line of 'The Queen threw a party for the whole country.' The rest followed and somehow I managed to provide her with the lyrics to both songs which she took from me as if it was simply the latest memo concerning the treatment of nits.

After lunch, the peacock strutted in again and thrust a bundle of furs at me like I had just made an exchange at an Indian trading camp.

'These are the outfits for the monologue,' she clucked, 'the Lion and Albert.'

Sure enough there was the cap for Albert, the fur coat for the lion, a zoo keeper's hat and enough old clobber to fit out the supporting cast.

'They know what to do, just make sure they get the delivery right.'

When the kids came in I copied her tactics and thrust the furs at the tallest, most sensible looking girl in the class and said, 'you know what to do with this lot.' They did too and they delivered a costumed monologue that had me clutching my ribs with laughter.

Towards the end of the afternoon the peacock strutted in with the rehashed version of *Jailhouse Rock* freshly typed and photocopied, one for each child.

'Get Gordon out,' she commanded, 'and let's give it a go.'

I was still a bit giggly after seeing 'The Lion and Albert' and when she said, 'Get Gordon out,' I imagined it to be something she often says to her knackered old husband after knocking back her third vodka and tonic.

Consequently, I had trouble singing through my chuckles.

Date: Thursday, 22.03.07
Location: St. Boswells
Today's Enemy: General Supply

There can be no beauty without ugliness, no grey without blue, no good without evil, and no joy without despair. I am home and it feels wonderful, a haven. The kettle is boiling and I am cutting a slice of walnut cake and for a while I am safe. I have been to St. Boswells and back and, like banging your head against a brick wall, it's great when it stops. I have actually developed a psychosomatic allergy to the place. As soon as I see it squatting across several fields I develop all the symptoms of flu. I get hot and shivery and develop headaches and just want to sleep. This is, of course, the classic symptoms of stress as first observed in the soldiers that fought in the first World War. It had been a day of 'general supply.'

'General Supply, please Sir, we are losing men and morale, the odds are overwhelming...'

'Get back in there, you lily-livered coward...'

The first hour involves a spot of invigilation where I just have to sit at the front of a sports hall and watch thirteen rows and fifteen columns of navy blue clad teenagers writing with tongue biting intensity. Even the most disaffected kids sit in quiescent mode obeying the principles and rituals of the great system. It's easy to be cynical, I can imagine Gerald Scarfe or Gertler sketching furiously at this picture of classic uniformity.

Sometimes, I wish I was bringing my sons up on a Micronesian island where they could swim all afternoon and sleep where they eventually fell under a moonlit sky using the warm tropical air for a blanket. Or even to take them travelling round the world in a recreational vehicle for a year. The nearest we get to that scheme is a visit to the annual Mobile Home show where we scurry in and out of the various vehicles and sit on the swivel seats and climb into the bed above the driver's seat and sit round the kitchen table and look out of the window at the spectacular scenery of the Grand Canyon.

The next lesson is history with Year 7. The actual classroom is an inspiration. A beacon to the bloody heroes who teach in these schools. A tribute to courage and conviction and a monument to those who transcend the everyday shit to soar like eagles and bring their lofty view to the little people down below. The walls are covered with work and I mean plastered and the ceiling too and now their usual teacher is having to peg their work up on crisscross clothes lines.

The class arrive, a raggedy crew of 12-year-olds. I know it's going to be tough when a boy, who looks as though he has spent his lunch break writhing in a pig pen, hands me over a grimy note which reads, 'Anthony has a wind problem and may need to go out of the classroom.' For the next hour, Anthony lived up to the letter and delighted in letting them rip. The reek was staggering and I mean putrid to the point where I was literally gagging. Of course, every time this happened the rest of the class called him a smelly cunt and a fucking dirty pig. Unfortunately, the only symptom of flu I did not have was a bunged up nose.

I am now convinced that the gods are toying with me. One of them is a Peter Ustinov look-a-like and is presently nibbling grapes from a daintily held bunch as he turns to Zeus and says in a breathy voice, 'let's see how he deals with the next task. Here it comes...'

'Please excuse Anthony, he has a bowel problem and may from time to time shit in your shoes.'

At lunchtime, I unwrap a sandwich and throw it in the bin, for some reason I have lost my appetite. Instead, I lie back on the vinyl and fall asleep to the sound of the fat women complaining bitterly about the length of time it takes to see a doctor, six weeks in her case. The conclusion is to make a doctor's appointment even if you are not ill, because by the time it comes up you probably will be. I am reminded of the Russian joke about the man who wanted to buy a car.

'When will it arrive?' he asks.

'In ten years,' replies the salesman.

'Will that be in the morning or the afternoon?'

'In the afternoon, why do you ask?'

'Because I have a plumber coming in the morning.'

I awake to the sound of the tea lady squealing for cups to be returned. The fat women are still piling rancour on their besieged GPs and the heat in the room is incredible. I am soaked through and red-faced. The weather has warmed up but the windows don't open and the central heating continues to pump it out unmercifully. I feel groggy and have to sit still until I come round as if from some major surgery. I really have to start questioning my existence because I am not happy. I have decided that enough is enough and Friday will be my last day here. I can't take anymore indignity, there are cases reaching the Hague that are weaker than mine.

The last lesson. I am to cover for a Year 9 bottom set in the computer room. The heat in this room is unreal. The last time I experienced anything approaching it was when I was a student working my vacation at the steel works making iron railway sleepers for the Nigerian government. I worked so close to the furnace that it was twenty minutes on, twenty minutes off with half a gallon of water in between but it was an igloo compared to this room. The class are bordering on thuggery and my flu symptoms are beginning to rage.

One girl threatens to kick my fucking balls up my back and looks as though she is capable of carrying out the threat. I can't be bothered pursuing her abuse because I am absolutely beat but there is still five minutes to go.

Unable or unwilling to hold the sea back any longer, I let them go and just manage to drag myself over to one side to avoid being trampled to death by hooves. I sit on the floor, sweat streaming down my forehead, looking up at a little twat from senior management with an intercom in his hand who is telling me that I have let them go four minutes early.

Date: Friday, 23.03.07
Location: St. Boswells
Today's Enemy: The System

Never has so much been owed by so many to so few. The end of term and a fortnight's respite and recuperation lies ahead, I can't call it a holiday because it will take the best part of it just to climb up to depletion point zero. As usual, the end of term is an anti-climax, a numbness of being. I have told them that after today I will not be back. I am 'going to Spain.' Every individual should be made to do one term in a city comprehensive school and that includes the public school future cabinet members so that they can have a taste of life through the mirror. Still, mustn't grumble because, as I've said before, grumbling is a coping mechanism. If you don't like it then get out. The English Department have given me a glowing reference. I take my hat off to the Head of the Department, a little feisty woman who loves her subject, her school and her kids with her heart and soul and who is afraid of no one regardless what size and attitude. However, she is leaving in summer and what then? There is no one in the department under fifty, a universal problem.

Today was decreed non-uniform day for the kids and by a quirk, the staff were expected to wear uniform. The kids just looked like kids but unfortunately some of the women staff just looked sad, I'm sorry but there it is. By all means, have a bit of light hearted fun, but not at the sacrifice of your dignity. Of course, it had to happen - St. Boswells being St. Boswells, all hell broke loose after lunch with fights and missile throwing and there in amongst it, trying to intervene, were three or four middle aged woman dressed like St. Trinian's school girls. They were ineffectual and the police had to be called. It kind of somehow sums it all up beautifully. Happy Easter.

At lunch time I lay across the sweaty black vinyl to drift away and thousands of bright shiny faces stared down like stars in the firmament. They had attained the peak of their own personal pyramid through help and guidance apportioned accordingly to each and every one of them. A little bit more spiritual healing here, a little bit more understanding there. Then all the faces smiled and said a simple thank you. Now it was my turn to smile and give thanks to them for helping me reach the top of my own personal pyramid.

The kids were never the enemy.

They were merely reacting to a system that was stifling the life out of their most precious and vital moments. A regime inflicted upon them by unenlightened governments since the days of Queen Victoria.

Under this system there would always be limited opportunities for spiritual exploration. The 'playing' fields are being sold off by the square foot and the creative and physical aspects of development are curtailed by an increasingly mechanistic, left-brained, male-orientated ideologically western approach that has resulted in a sea of dissatisfaction, underachievement and the ensuing development of alienated subcultures.

Recently I spoke to a class of 16-year-olds who were only three weeks away from leaving school. It quickly became obvious that the system had failed this particular group terribly. They had been badly let down and were being released from captivity unable to fend for themselves in the wild. I asked them how much an average terraced house cost and the answers ranged between £8,000 and £35,000. The term mortgage meant nothing. Their financial naivety was staggering and would soon leave them victim to the circling sharks of store finance and plastic credit.

Their knowledge of careers was virtually non-existent, apart from the obvious ones of beautician and car mechanic. The possibilities of becoming anything from actuary to zoologist had completely bypassed them.

Their knowledge of sex was probably explicit due to unmonitored access to the internet but it seemed that no great emphasis had been placed on discussing what makes a relationship work. The statistic that two of the girls would be pregnant within 18 months was conveniently shunted into oblivion along with any pre-emptive advice on childcare.

They all smoked, took drugs, lived on a diet of crisps, coke, burgers and chocolate and were predominately either stick thin or dangerously overweight. Most had never prepared a meal or been involved in any domestic chores. Simple DIY jobs such as rewiring a plug or fixing a toilet were destined to remain a mystery. The concept of exercise was laughed out of the room and their knowledge of current affairs was limited to celebrity spats.

Sometimes, it feels foolish to ask them to turn to page 42, the paragraph; 'Mr Darcy returns.' It's a wonderful thing to be introduced to great novels and works of art and for that introduction to lead to a passionate affair but throughout history it has never been productive to place the horse in front of the cart. We had failed them and thousands of others by not encouraging and reinforcing their own concepts of individually and self-belief. We the teachers, as part of the system, had only added more choking layers of indoctrination around their original curious and questioning minds when we should have been trying to leave them open to self-discovery, peeling away our own layers in the process.

The teachers aren't to blame. (Well, not all of them.) The system created divisions within the ranks and destroyed any notions of a cohesive force and subsequent cooperative behaviour. Instead, the powers that be fashioned industrial model Senior Management Teams that led to everyone looking over their shoulder. A system that nurtured a McCarthyist approach to help and guidance where your colleague was forced to monitor your lessons and then pass their comments on your performance to the dreaded SMT, creating a dog-eat-dog culture and a controlling ethos where the doctrine states: 'It is easier to control the individual than the group.' The extended picture shows the teachers fragmenting themselves into several different unions. 'United, we are strong. Divided, we fall.' Repeat after me…

It is a system that moves under the feet like a thinly crusted swamp at the arrival of the most recent directive from the latest Education Minister wishing to make an impact. The average time spent in this ministerial outpost is two years, which is truly contemptuous of any principles of stability and consistency. An example can be seen in the approach to language teaching in this country. Last year it was decreed acceptable for 14-year-olds to drop a foreign language. This year the government have decided that languages must be taught in Primary Schools. This is the D'oh! system of education. They have finally got round to realising that as far as languages are concerned the younger a person starts to learn it the easier it will be for them to understand. Incidentally, two-year-old French kids don't learn long lists of declensions first. All you overworked primary school teachers have three months to become bi-lingual, but don't panic because next month the idea will have been scotched for something even more fantastical.

There was hope, however. I recently spent some time teaching a group of 14-year-olds who were educated in a Steiner school before moving to mainstream education to complete their exams. Whatever methods had been employed by Steiner had created pleasant-mannered young people with seemingly no axe to grind. It was a case of putting people before process: Steiner schools educate the 'whole child' through hands-on learning, placing a strong emphasis on creativity. It all sounds quite hippy, like the Montessori method that was popular in the 60s and 70s and still around today, but you can't argue with results. One Steiner school in southern England is being assessed for city academy status, and an inner-city Manchester school is being given £40,000 to experiment with the Montessori method. If both or even either were successful, it could open the way for others. One government-appointed professor explains, "Steiner schools are one example where you don't have tests." But they still develop the capability of pupils so that they are able to take GCSEs and go into further or higher education. "That seems to say you don't have to do it by tests and targets. You can do it through a more human relationship between teachers and pupils...State school children are entering the system at one end and emerging at the other with a clutch of grades but too often little else. Not everything that goes into turning a child into a well-rounded adult can be measured. Too much education policy assumes it can."

I must have been shouting and twitching and kicking out in my angst-ridden coma because I was shaken back to semi-consciousness by a snaggle-toothed dinner lady. I don't remember much of what happened on that last day, only that I was hastily stretchered onto a hovering chopper and as we climbed I saw the screaming hordes appear from out of the flattened elephant grass. Then someone put a cigar stub in my mouth and I stared into oblivion through tired eyes as Samuel Barber's *Adagio For Strings* faded in around me.

Gone to Spain